Embroidery

AROUNNA KHOUNNORAJ

a modern guide to botanical embroidery

photography by Lauren Kolyn

Hardie Grant

QUADRILLE

Contents

Introduction

There was a time when many young people practised the art of embroidery by making samplers and other projects as part of their life skills training. But, in hindsight, these were much more than just training exercises to develop design skills or hand/eye coordination; they were ways to pass on from generation to generation the traditions and expressions that define who we are. Embroidery has been a part of every culture from prehistory to the present day. And while its roots may have been utilitarian – patching, mending and reinforcing – it grew and evolved to encompass design elements, techniques and stitchwork that reflect ever more decorative and expressive possibilities. In fact today embroidery defines such a large category of needlework that it is hard to know where it begins or ends. But, simply put, it is the art of decorating fabric using needle and thread, embellishing a surface with a myriad of stitches to build, from line alone, a wealth of pattern, image, colour and texture.

I, too, learned embroidery when I was young, although perhaps not in such a rigorous way as previous generations. Upon arrival in Canada my mother trained as a seamstress and, as a young immigrant family, sewing, making and mending were always a part of our household. So, along with general sewing skills, I took it all in and it remained with me all the way through art schools, residencies as a fibre artist and into my studio. In a lifetime of working with textiles, embroidery was always one of my favourite techniques; it was my way of drawing on fabric using only thread, building patterns or creating images expressed in colour, line and shape. It was a way of adding layers and detail to whatever it was that I was making, whether paper goods, production bags or large artistic pieces – even sculpture.

But I think that it's not enough to view embroidery as just an element of work. For me it has proven to be a core activity, but one that embodies much more. It has become a way to unify all my artistic practices precisely because its techniques, applications and materiality directly relate to so many other activities – mending, fashion work, punch needle and quilting to name only a few. So, no matter where my work took me, no matter how diverse my interests, embroidery was somehow always present. And like many of those activities, embroidery inherently expresses the very idea of handwork: compositions that reflect my thought process, sitting and working on a piece of cloth, applying designs stitch by stitch, line by line, back and forth in colourful and textured additions. It is a quiet process, meditative, thinking with my hands with the simplest of tools at my fingertips.

History shows that most embroidery exists somewhere between the more structured 'counted threads' technique, where patterns and repetitions are based on the weave of the base cloth, and a more 'free–style' technique, where embroidery work is limited only by how you want to express your design. My approach to embroidery is similar to the way I draw and, I think, is consistent with a more modern approach. I enjoy the freedom of drawing designs any way I like and letting the stitchwork express itself in any combination. And, as someone who loves to keep busy, embroidery is something I always keep with me wherever I am. I often have my well-worn sewing kit with me, stuffed with threads, needles and cloth, so I can continue working for a few moments while sitting in a park or travelling. Small patterns, insects or miniature gardens – anything that I might see or imagine – can be created on the go.

How to use this book

——

Embroidery is something that I can combine with any number of studio activities. Much of my work has focused on handmade objects of a utilitarian nature such as purses, personal accessories and home goods. I love useful things. But that's not to say that I don't appreciate more artistic pursuits and projects that have no other purpose than to illustrate the beauty of a technique or material. And I've found that embroidery perfectly embraces these two ideas, always suitable as a complement to any sewing project I might be working on, but also completely able to stand on its own, expressing its beauty in and of itself.

My intention in this book is to guide you through embroidery techniques that will be useful for anything that you may be inspired to do, as well as through specific projects from my studio that I hope you will find inspiring. As such, I've organized the book into two main sections – stitches and projects – with both sections working in conjunction with each other to focus on both the details of individual stitches and on projects that highlight each stitch, individually and in different combinations. In both sections I've included descriptions and thoughts on how I've used different stitches, as well as step-by-step drawings and illustrations for you to follow along and refer to. So, as you work through a project, you will also be referred to the Stitch Directory (see page 27) for specific instructions on how to work the stitches used in the project.

One of the difficulties in describing embroidery is the sheer number of techniques that have been handed down to us from different times and different places. Add to that the neverending combinations and variations and the list becomes quite long and complex. So, rather than create a compendium of stitch techniques, I've focused on many of my favourites, the stitches that I use regularly and that have a range of qualities and characteristics for any type of work that you might do – some simple, some more complex. Although I'm a big believer in working intuitively and using your own creative freedom, I've organized the stitches into generally accepted groups based on how different stitches are typically used: those best suited for linear elements; borders; filler stitches; and those that are more free-style and ornamental. Similarly, I've organized the projects into three different groups: projects for the home, useful and decorative items for your life; wearable items such as clothing and accessories; and art pieces that combine embroidery with different media. There are projects at different skill levels, so there will be something for everyone.

On the following pages I've included descriptions of all the different tools and materials that you might need, as well as all the necessary steps to start your projects – from choosing your materials, designing and transferring your image, selecting colours and threads and stretching and working with your hoop. You can download the project templates at www.bookhou.com/pages/embroidery-patterns, if you don't feel comfortable drawing them freehand. At the end of the book, you will also find a resource guide to help you locate some of the suppliers of equipment tools and embroidery threads.

Tools and materials

Embroidery has been around for centuries, and its one constant is the fundamental relationship between a fabric base, a thread and a needle. That relationship might sound simple, but it gets a little more complex because, whatever you do, tools matter. And for every job there is a tool. Different threads need different needles, as do different fabrics. Along with all the creative possibilities within embroidery there are many tools and materials as well, both commonplace and specialized. Each is purposed to work in a specific way to achieve specific results. So it can sometimes be confusing, especially when there is more than one choice for any project. However, the items that you will need can be reduced to a well-chosen few.

Needles

Despite their small size, needles are one of the most important tools you will use when you are embroidering. They are what joins fabric to thread and each has specific characteristics, so which one you choose will be determined by the cloth and the threads you will be using. Considering whether your cloth is dense or not, with a higher or lower thread count, and also the thickness of your thread, will help you determine the most suitable needle for you. There are several types of needle that are typically used in embroidery, each with a different point, shaft size and eye size. Within each type there are also different lengths, some more suitable to specific tasks than others. Numbering systems are the same as those governing wire gauges, so the smaller the number the larger the needle, and the larger the number the smaller the needle.

When choosing needles there are some general guidelines to keep in mind. When doing fine detailed work slightly shorter needles can

sometimes give you more hand control, while the ability to load your needle for faster straight stitches might call for a longer needle. This is also determined by what feels comfortable in your hand. In addition, choose a point suitable for the fabric you are using, and an eye sized for the thread – but one that will not create too large a hole that may mar your work. An elongated eye rather than a wider eye is better in this case.

Along with your needles you might want to use a needle threader to help you thread the needle quickly. I also like to have a needle minder close by – a metal pin that is magnetic, so I always know where my needle is and it's not lost on the floor or chair. You may also want a place to store your needles to keep them from getting dull; I use a needle book and you can also store them in a tube.

EMBROIDERY NEEDLE
Embroidery needles are extremely versatile. They are similar to general sewing needles (sharps) in that they are typically medium in length with a sharp tip capable of piercing tightly woven fabric, but with a larger and longer eye to accommodate multiple strands of thread. They usually range from sizes 1 to 10 (with 1 being the largest), which refers to both the overall length and the eye size/length. The most common uses call for sizes 6 to 8.

TAPESTRY NEEDLE
Tapestry needles have a blunt tip and larger eyes, generally for use with open or loosely woven fabrics and for doing counted thread types of embroidery or cross stitch. The blunt rounded tip won't pierce the fabric but rather will go in between the strands, while the larger eye will fit a higher number of strands as well as thicker wool threads. These needles are sized

from 13 to 28 – 13 being the largest – referring to the thickness of the needle and the eye size. A typical size for embroidery tends to be around 24, but this is more suitable for cloth with looser weaves and lower thread counts.

CHENILLE NEEDLE

Chenille needles are similar to embroidery needles in that they have sharp tips but also a larger, longer eye. The sharp point allows the needle to pierce tightly woven fabric and the larger eye can accommodate thicker yarns such as wool, or even ribbon. These needles tend to be a bit shorter in length than embroidery needles and are typically sized from 13 to 28. They are good for doing crewel embroidery or other wool work with thicker yarns.

MILLINER'S NEEDLE

Milliner's needles are longer needles with a sharp end but with a narrow eye that doesn't expand too much beyond the width of the needle. Because of this they can pierce tightly woven fabric, but they tend to be used with thinner groupings of threads such as when making decorative stitches, bullion knots or French knots, where the thread is wrapped around the shaft and the needle is passed through the wraps. Typical sizes range from 1 to 10, plus 15 and 18.

DARNING NEEDLE

Darning needles are in some sense similar to tapestry needles except perhaps a little longer. They have a dull rounded tip, making them suitable for working with yarns and repairing knitted items. They generally aren't considered an embroidery needle but I found that they do have a place when doing stitching like picot, where a needle with a dull tip is useful. If you don't have one nearby you can use the eye end of the needle instead.

Embroidery threads

There are many kinds of embroidery thread (also called embroidery floss) available in many different materials, each with their own qualities. Which ones you choose can depend on different factors, such as the nature of the fabric you are using and what effects you hope to achieve with the stitches. In many respects, there are no hard and fast rules, so a fair amount of experimentation is sometimes necessary to find your favourite.

There are a few starting points though. Most embroidery thread can be described by type of fibre, its weight and how the fibres are twisted together to make the thread. The most common threads tend to be one of two types: non-divisible or divisible. Non-divisible threads are made by tightly twisting together two or more strands and are meant to be used as they are; divisible threads are made of strands that can be separated from one another.

COTTON THREAD

The different types of cotton thread are made of the same cotton fibres but differ in how they are composed. This, in turn, gives each type certain qualities in feel and appearance that give you choices as to how you can use them. The two types both have their benefits, but they can also easily be combined.

Stranded cotton or floss is a divisible thread typically made of six loosely-twisted strands that can be separated into smaller groups of strands depending on the thickness of thread you want. It is a very versatile thread because the thickness can be varied to suit your design. Individual strands can be used for very fine work, although stranded cotton can lose strength as a single strand. Larger groups of strands can be used for increasingly bigger stitches, to work on large areas economically. Different thicknesses of thread also allow you to create linear designs with line thicknesses that vary depending on how many strands you use. Stranded cotton is also softer in appearance, and more painterly. Individual stitches tend not to stand out but instead appear as a smooth continuous surface, which makes it perfect for stitches such as satin, split or short and long. Stranded cotton comes in skeins of 8m (8¾yd), and in a wide range of colours. It can be dull or glossy in appearance, although most types are treated with a process to give it some degree of gloss. It is usual practice to separate the strands, or strip out, before laying them back together again for stitching – this gives them a neater appearance, but that's up to you.

The other type of thread is the non-divisible. This is a large category that consists of several common threads that are made of tightly twisted strands of cotton – or sometimes silk – and which cannot be separated out into individual strands. Common types are perlé (pearl) cotton, which

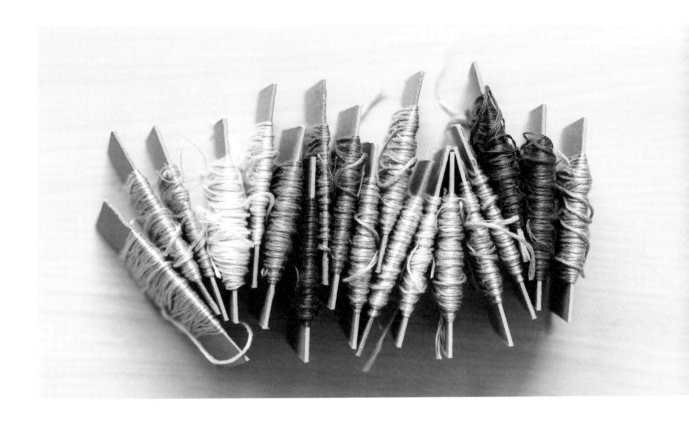

is made with two strands, coton à broder, which is made with five strands, and floche, which is made with four strands. In addition to the number of strands, these threads tend to come in a variety of weights or thicknesses that approximate the different thicknesses created by separating stranded thread. Perlé cotton is rope-like with a discernible form and texture, so individual stitches tend to stand out – which makes it perfect if you want to do a project with one specific thread width to give the design consistency, or when you want a thread line to have a strong visual weight and a clean appearance. Non-divisible thread can come in skeins or longer lengths in balls and usually has a glossy finish.

OTHER NATURAL THREADS
You can also use silk and wool embroidery threads – both crewel and tapestry. Silk is a lovely thread to work, with an amazing luminous quality that works nicely with techniques that have a blended look. Wool threads come in a variety of weights as well as a degree of fineness and can add a lovely textural quality to your work. Crewel, a wool thread that is not unlike the twisted

cottons, is smooth compared to its wool tapestry cousin, and can be used equally on linen as on knitwear. Tapestry wool, by comparison, is thicker and heavier – not unlike yarn – but offers a nice contrast. I have recently started using wool for embroidery because I like the dull look that wool offers as opposed to the satin quality of cotton threads.

There is also a myriad of other threads made from rayon or polyester, metallic threads and coils, as well as blends and even ribbon or thin strands of cut fabric – all of which can be a lovely addition to any project.

For the projects in this book I used DMC and Sajou stranded cotton as well as perlé cotton and wool threads from Wonderfil. For the felt patches I used gold work bullion wire, which is held in place with couching stitches. For each project I have identified which brand and colour I used, but feel free to use what you have on hand.

Base cloth

There are many types of fabric that you can embroider on, but not all fabrics are equal and they can produce varying results. Different types of base cloth can have very different qualities; the type of fibres and weave, the weight and texture, and colour and feel all contribute to their suitability. There are a couple of key questions you need to ask to help determine what fabric is right for any given project: what is the nature of the project – is it artistic or functional, fine or utilitarian; and what kind of stitching do you want to use – the geometry of counted thread or the organic lines of free-form design? Knowing this will help you consider the qualities you need in a base cloth: the weight, type of weave and thread count, smooth or textured, and the nature of its fibres, natural or synthetic. Some of these qualities are merely a matter of choice and aesthetics, but others can determine how you work. Working with different weights is also possible, but may call for adjustments. Heavier cottons like canvas are great for projects that call for more resilience, but can be tough to stitch and can fray your thread; working with a thinner thread and needle and a thimble might be better. Using heavier fabrics with more texture is also a design issue because they may overpower your embroidery. Working with lighter weight fabric or lower thread counts might be fine for certain stitches, but for other situations you may need to strengthen thinner fabric with a backing cloth such as cotton calico (muslin) – which is also a fine fabric to embroider on.

Because I embroider the way I draw, with botanical elements and free-form compositions, I use plenty of circular and curved elements, with a variety of stitch types. I like combinations of open areas as well as denser, tightly worked areas, delicate lines and filled-in areas. And I quite often work my embroidery into sewing projects. So, with all that in mind, I personally gravitate to natural fabrics, such as cotton and especially linen, usually in medium weights. I find these fabrics, whether 100% or blends and which are woven with a single strand and a tighter weave, to be the most suitable fabrics for the type of surface embroidery that I do. The weave is even and full without the gaps of open-weave fabrics. They are often stiff enough to stretch easily on a hoop or frame, generally smooth without too much texture, and have a high enough thread count to support an array of stitches. They also come in a full range of colours and I love the look of them. If you're unsure, the best thing is to try a test piece with the embroidery stitches you want to use. I would also suggest trying some samples of fabric before investing in larger amounts. You can also practise on pre-made fabrics such as napkins, clothing or pillowcases. As you make more pieces you will develop your own taste and know what you enjoy using.

LINEN

The fibres of linen are slightly irregular, which gives it a very natural look. Not all linens are equal in quality, but generally linen is one of those fabrics that is equally suitable for any type of embroidery, and it's also a perfect fabric for sewing. Linens tend to fall into two types: 'even weave', meaning that both the warp and weft are roughly equal in thread count; and 'plain weave' where the thread count may not be equal, but it is generally high and visually fuller. Even-weave linen quite often has prominent open spaces within the weave that are useful for counted thread types of stitchwork, while plain weave is smooth, without obvious openings between threads. If you enjoy working in a free-style manner with compositions full of curves and shapes that don't refer to the grid of the fabric, then plain-weave linen is for you. It's smooth, but with some texture, it stretches evenly without too much movement, and comes in a variety of colours. It is sold by weight rather than stitch count, but any number of weights can be suitable for different projects.

COTTON FABRICS

Cotton calico (muslin) is also a favourite of mine. Its threads are lighter than linen but it has a higher thread count – between 80 to 130 is a good range when choosing a base for embroidery. It is also a suitable backing, providing extra body and structure when the base fabric is too lightweight. For some projects, such as bags, I use heavier fabrics like canvas, which can be more resistant to wear and tear but can be harder to work with because of the heavier weight and tighter weave.

WOOL AND CRAFT FELT

Wool/craft felt has a lovely texture to sew on and is pretty much accepting of anything you want to try with it. Any type of needle, thicker or thinner, works well because the felted surface allows it to pass through without difficulty. The softness of the wool also makes the stitches seem debossed, giving the work depth and an object-like quality. It's one of my favourite fabrics to use for patches, pins or appliqué because it provides a stiff surface. Also it doesn't fray, so it can be cut into shapes and the edges left raw, and it comes in plenty of colours. I like black which can really highlight the embroidery.

READY-MADE ITEMS

There are several other fabric choices that are equally usable for embroidery projects, including ready-made items such as napkins and towels to shirts and sweaters. Not only is embroidery on ready-made items a great way to upcycle pieces but it adds a lovely pattern and motif.

Hoops and frames

Hoops and frames have two main purposes: to stretch your cloth and keep it in taut while you work; and to give you something to hold onto while you are working, particularly if the piece is small. There is also perhaps a third purpose, if we include its role as a possible frame for presenting your finished work. Like most things, there are a few mainstays on the market and many choices in terms of quality. Typically they range from hand-held hoops and smaller stretcher frames to tabletop stretching frames for larger work.

HOOPS

Simple hoops tend to be plastic, bamboo, plywood or hardwood. These are commonly available and work when an outer ring tightens around an inner ring, with the cloth in between. Inexpensive ones have thumbscrews for tightening, better ones have sturdier hardware holding thumbscrews combined with a slot for a screwdriver. I find those small screws hard to tighten and to be able to use a screwdriver to tighten helps a lot. To improve your hoop's grip it is common to wrap the inside ring, and sometimes both, in a tight wrapping of fabric; this also reduces any marks that may result from stretching. I tend to use no-slip hoops a fair amount. They are plastic but have an inner channel that allows the rings to lock together, providing a tight grip on your fabric. They come in a variety of sizes, but I find working with a smaller hoop more comfortable, because I quite often hold my hoops in my hand while working.

FRAMES

There are a number of frames, from inexpensive to not so inexpensive. On the lesser side are square plastic frames that can easily be assembled and reused, which is ideal for storing and travelling. They are good for not leaving very noticeable frame marks, but I find that they take some practise to use. On the higher end there are several tabletop frames that provide adjustable tension and still allow you to work on larger pieces. Or you can make up a simple homemade frame using wood stretcher bars; simply stretch your fabric using a staple gun to attach it to the wood. This also makes it a good way to display the piece after you use it as a working frame.

Transfer equipment

There are many ways to transfer your design onto your base cloth and a number of products available to help, ranging from simple and direct to more complex (see page 18 for transfer techniques).

TRANSFER PENCILS/PENS

The simplest method is to use an ordinary pencil and draw directly on the cloth. I tend to use softer pencils so that the line is dark enough to see but not too dark, but it's good to have an array of hardnesses for different colours and weights of fabric. Micron pens are also excellent pens to draw on fabric as they are thin and permanent. If your cloth is dark you can use a white pencil, chalk pencil or even thin white gel pens. There are times you might not want the pencil to show through the threads, in which case a heat-erasable pen – which creates lines that will disappear with heat – or chalk pencils – which create lines that can be rubbed off or rinsed under water – are the answer. There are also a few heat transfer pens on the market. They can be used to draw your design onto paper, which is then placed right side down on the fabric and ironed to transfer the design onto the fabric. These are non-washable but come in a variety of colours.

TRANSFER PAPERS

Transfer papers are sometimes useful when your fabric is too heavy to see through for direct tracing with a light source (see page 18). Transfer papers come in several forms – for instance, simple graphite paper, which has a coat of graphite on thin paper that is transferred to your fabric when you draw on the back. Lines can sometimes be faint though, so using it on light, smooth fabric is best. You can also make your own transfer paper by redrawing your pattern on the back of your pattern with a soft pencil. It can then be transferred to your cloth with an iron or by rubbing.

Water soluble paper like Sulky Stick 'n Stitch is a great product that you can draw on with a pencil or permanent marker and peel and stick onto the cloth. The paper stays in place as you embroider directly through the paper into your fabric. Once your piece is done, run the paper under water and the paper will dissolve. This product is good for very detailed images or if you're working on a darker base cloth. It can also be put through your home printer if you don't want to draw on the paper.

Makers of printing paper make a heat transfer product that you iron onto cloth. This is a good way to transfer a coloured image or photograph onto your base cloth, which you can then stitch on top of or use as a guide for your embroidery. This is a good alternative to having your image digitally printed and you will have control of which fabric you want the transfer on. It isn't useful as a general transfer technique though, because the product remains in place so will be visible between your stitches.

Scissors

Having a good pair of snips or embroidery scissors on hand for cutting your threads while you work and cleaning up afterwards is absolutely necessary. The tip needs to be sharp and small to get into tight areas of your work. You will also need a pair of fabric scissors to cut down fabric. Pinking shears are fabric scissors that cut a zigzag line, which helps prevent fraying and can be good as a finishing cut.

Other items

There are several other items that are always useful to have in your sewing box.

Masking tape, or any other kind of tape, is helpful for holding down drawings or templates while tracing.

Rulers are also handy when cutting and framing.

Pins are a staple that should always be within reach. When you're adding appliqué to your work and need to hold down pieces of fabric before you embroider on top, or when you're sewing layers together, pins will keep things from shifting and moving. If you don't like using pins a paper glue stick is also great for temporarily holding things together before tacking (basting) or sewing.

A thimble is great at keeping your fingertip from getting sore when you're doing a lot of sewing and embroidery work, especially with thicker fabric.

An iron is good to have for those times you want to do image transfer or for giving everything a nice press at the end.

A small watercolour set is a good way to experiment with colour and design before you set off with an embroidery project. You can even paint with watercolour on fabric, then embroider on top.

Basic techniques

This section covers some of the basic techniques that you will use again and again. However, I should mention that it is not always possible to prepare each project in the same way. One important question is whether to stretch your base cloth before you transfer your drawing, or the other way around. Ideally, I prefer to prepare my fabric and then stretch it before I transfer my design. But this is not always possible, such as when you are using a small hoop and working on small areas within a larger design, in which case you need to be mindful when stretching to avoid distorting your drawing.

Preparing your fabric

For most fabrics it is a good idea to pre-wash them before using so all the starch is removed, and they are soft to the hand. Pre-washing is also important if you use Sulky Stick 'n Stitch to avoid any shrinkage after you rinse your work to remove the paper. If the base fabric shrinks any amount after you finish your embroidery, the stitches may pucker. Once you have determined your pattern, thread colours and base cloth, the next step is to transfer your image.

Transferring the image

There are many methods that can be used, depending on the fabric you are using as a base cloth and the nature of the project that you will be making. The method I most often use to transfer the image is to draw freehand directly onto the cloth with either a hard pencil (see images on page 14) or with a heat-sensitive pen so the lines will disappear when the fabric is ironed. I like to use a pencil when working on a light-coloured base cloth and I don't often worry about the line showing through because I usually stitch over it. If the fabric is dark you can use

a white or coloured pencil (see image opposite). If your base cloth is light enough in colour and weight, you can transfer your drawing using a window or light box as a light source. Print your image to size, then place the template under the fabric and hold it in place with tape or pins. Make sure that you place the template completely flat on the cloth so that you will be able to see the lines better. Holding the pieces up to a window, or on a light box, trace the image with a pencil or heat-sensitive pen.

If your base cloth is too opaque to see through, you can use a transfer paper such as graphite paper. Print your image to the size needed. Place your base cloth flat on a table right side up. Place the transfer paper right side down on top (transfer paper has a shiny side and dull side and the shiny side should be the side next to the fabric) and the template on top of the transfer paper right side up. Trace along the lines of the template using a pen or pencil and the transfer paper will transfer the image onto the cloth. In many cases these lines will erase or wash off, or you can stitch over them. Transfer paper comes in different colours so you can trace onto a light or dark base cloth.

If the template design is highly detailed, print the image to size onto water soluble Sulky Stick 'n Stitch paper, which works like a sticker and will adhere to the base cloth. Following the instructions, place it where you want and then begin your embroidery by stitching right through the paper onto the cloth. When finished, rinse the Sulky paper under warm water, gently rubbing until it dissolves. I sometimes have small leftover pieces of the paper that won't fit through a printer, but I use a permanent marker to draw on them to use for other projects, especially small ones like the mini hoops or pins.

Using tacking (basting) stitches is a simple way to transfer an image onto a dark base cloth, using a photocopy of your design or a drawing on paper or tracing paper. Place the drawing or photocopy on top of your base cloth right side up. With a needle and contrasting coloured thread, sew along the lines of your design with large stitches. You can keep it as a simple shape or add as much detail as you can. Once done, tear the paper away. Embroider on top of the stitched lines, removing them after you have finished the embroidery, if necessary.

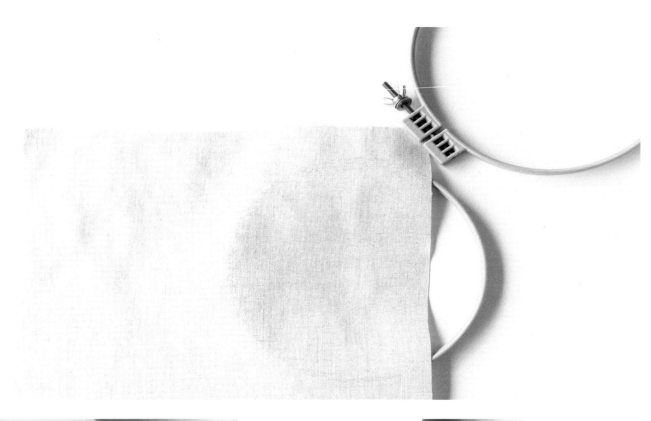

Using a stretching hoop or frame

Although there are many ways to stretch your base cloth, I mostly use hoops and wood frames to work on. Hoops come in two parts with an inner ring around which an outer ring clamps to hold your embroidery in place. A wood stretcher frame is assembled and the cloth is stapled in place.

Before framing, press your embroidered fabric from the reverse side with a hot iron and using a pressing cloth. This helps give your piece a nice smooth finish.

If the piece is quite small, a simple wood hoop is fine. If you are using a larger wood hoop you might want to prepare it by wrapping fabric strips around the entire inner ring to create a tighter grip on your base cloth. For larger pieces I tend to use Morgan No-Slip Hoops because they are easy to use and hold the cloth tight, due to the indented channel on the exterior hoop that allows the interior hoop to lock into place. Quite often, though, I will use a wood hoop as the presentation hoop.

To stretch a fabric in a hoop, lay your cloth flat on a table right side up and place the inner hoop underneath, making sure that the area of the design that you want to work on is within the ring. Place the outer hoop on top of the fabric with the tightening screw in a location where it won't get in the way when holding the hoop. Before you press the outer ring down, make sure there is enough fabric all the way around so that you can pull it taut. Quite often you may have to work on a larger piece of cloth and trim it to the final size after completion.

Press the outer ring down over the inner ring and tighten the screw until it is snug but not too tight. Stretching the fabric is a combination of pulling the fabric down little by little on all sides, while alternately tightening the hoop. Make sure to go all around the perimeter so the fabric is completely flat with equal tension all round. While everyone has a preference for how they work on a hoop, I find that it is much easier to work on one that is as tight as possible – I find that it makes stitching easier; if the hoop is not tight it's a little like jumping on a trampoline. You may need to readjust and retighten your hoop if you find that you have issues with tension while working.

The other type of frame I use for projects is a wood stretcher frame, which can double as a working frame and as a presentation frame. While there are a number of commercial wood frames available, mine tend to be simple homemade versions using four pieces of 2.5 x 5-cm (1 x 2-in) pine, glued and nailed. Make sure that your fabric has an extra 10–12.5cm (4–5in) on all sides so that there's enough material to hold onto and staple to the back of the frame. To begin, place your fabric flat on a table, right side down. Place the frame on top of the fabric with the area you want to work on in the middle. Start by stapling the cloth taut at the middle point of all four sides. Then work from the middle towards the corners by stretching with one hand and stapling with the other every 2.5cm (1in) or so. Staple a few on one side, then rotate to the next side. Keep repeating until all sides are secure. As you pull the cloth tight, make sure it is firm but not so tight so that the weave of the fabric becomes warped or distorted. When you get to the corners, fold it in a diagonal line like a hospital bed corner and staple it down.

1.

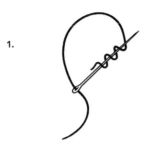

2.

3.

4.

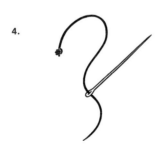

Starting and finishing

In most cases I start and end my stitches with a knotted thread, although when I am couching a thicker thread or rope I fold the loose end back upon itself and tie it down with a couching stitch. In general I try to keep my knots neat and trim any extra loose threads. It's a good idea to end the stitches when necessary, rather than having long lines of thread running on the underside of your embroidery. While the underside can be a little messy if it doesn't show, it's better to keep it clean – especially if your cloth is lightweight so you can see the direction lines of the threads through it.

QUILTER'S KNOT
Always cut thread an arm's length and no longer, or it may tangle as you work.

1. Place the tail on the top edge of the needle and with the other hand pinch the tip. Wrap the thread around the needle several times – how many times determines how big the knot will be.
2. Pinch the wrapped thread with the same finger and push it towards the eye of the needle. As you get to the eye, gently begin to release a bit of your grip.
3. Pull the wraps down until you reach the bottom of the thread – what you are doing is pulling the knot and needle away from each other in opposite directions
4. You'll end up with a neat knot at the end of the thread.

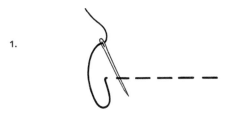

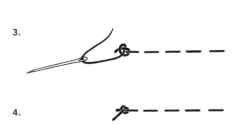

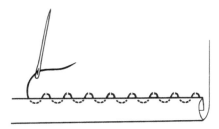

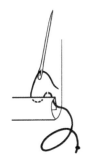

FINISHING KNOT

This is used at the end of a length of hand sewing on the underside of the fabric.

1. Turn your work over so you are working on the back of the fabric, with the needle and thread on this side. Take your needle under the last stitch on this side and pull the thread until a loop forms.
2. Pass the needle through the loop.
3. Pull until a knot is formed. To secure the knot further you can repeat the steps for a larger knot if you prefer.
4. Clip the thread end to 5mm (¼in).

BLIND STITCH

This stitch is used to close openings because the tiny stitches are almost invisible on the right side of the fabric.

1. Thread your needle and make a quilter's knot at the end (see page 22). Bring the needle up through one folded edge so the knot will be hidden inside. Take a tiny stitch though the opposite layer of fabric, so it will be invisible on the right side, then take a longer stitch through the folded edge.
2. Continue in this way along the open edge until you have closed the gap, then fasten off.

TOP STITCHING

This is a line of stitching, usually done on a sewing machine, that is worked near an edge on the right side to give a crisp finish. It can be just decorative or at the same can close a gap in the edge seam.

Design process

Inspiration

I find inspiration in many places, one of them being nature. Even though I live in an urban city there are pockets of green throughout – parks and ravines, but also gardens and overgrown alleyways. I think that inspiration is something that you don't necessarily seek out, it's all around you; all you have to do is look and interpret what you see. One of my favourite things to do is to collect bits of nature and use them as inspiration for drawings. The shapes you draw don't have to be exact replicas but they are good to have for a reference. I usually tape the pieces to the wall and let them dry so I can take a glance when I feel I need to study them. Keeping a sketchbook is a nice way to jot down ideas and thoughts and you will find it to be a great resource whenever you look back – or have a pin board of collected images you find in magazines or online. These will all become places that you can turn to when you are trying to figure out a design.

I like to combine bits of colour for my work with watercolour painting or drawing on my tablet. I find that working out my colours can save a lot of time and give me an overall feel for the piece before starting with the stitching. I also find that before you start on a big project or try stitches you haven't used before, it's a good idea to create little samples that will give you practise without the pressure of working on the finished piece. These samples will help you to make design decisions quickly rather than applying the ideas on a larger scale and making changes as you go.

I don't think that you have to do these steps – but I find that when I plan out the ideas and design of a piece beforehand, in the end I save a lot of time and sometimes frustration. During the stitching process you will make modifications and adjustments as you progress and that's okay. I don't think it's a straightforward path and I personally enjoy this development process.

Selecting colours

Choosing what colours to use for your projects is probably one of the most consistently difficult tasks. Even though you may try to work them out in advance, it never quite works – making adjustments along the way just seems to be part of the process. But making as many decisions as you can before you start is always helpful, especially when it comes to colour. When I work there are times when I use only one or two colours to emphasize a design's lines, shapes or texture – I find this is my preferred approach when stitching patterns. But other times – when my design is more pictorial, such as with a botanical motif – I will choose a range of colours that work well together, and contribute to a certain aesthetic.

In selecting colours you are choosing a palette, a combination of colours that fulfills your compositional needs. Many are subjective, consisting of personal choices and favourites, which is perfectly fine. Some palettes consist of a bounty of colours, while others are reduced to a few, sometimes monochromatic or even a single colour. Some can be light or dark. There are really no hard rules for choosing a palette, but there are some things to think about when choosing colour combinations. To get a sense of this, it's useful to think about colour in general. Primary colours – red, blue and yellow – when mixed, result in secondary colours: purple, green and orange. When arranged on a colour wheel, primaries and secondaries can, in turn, be mixed to create an array of tertiary colours: different reds, oranges, blues and so forth. In addition, every colour can be modified to various degrees in terms of light or dark. Pure colours or hues when mixed with white produce tints, when mixed with black create shades, and when mixed with grey make tones. In real life this might all add up to billions of different colours. But, thankfully, thread colours typically just come in the hundreds.

One of the takeaways here is that it's not just colours we are looking for but also a whole range of lights and darks as well. One way to organize all the hues, tints, shades and tones is to think of them as families. A family might consist of one pure-ish colour along with two or three variations, some lighter, some darker. A palette might consist of three or four families, some with similarities such as warmth, and some with contrasting qualities as well. In the end you may not use them all, but there will be enough to let each element in your design stand out. The beauty of embroidery and its visual strength is truly evident when the larger design elements work in conjunction with its smallest: the individual stitch. Nothing gets lost. The colour combinations you choose are one way to achieve this. First, using a variety of tones of any single colour will avoid the flatness of simple colours, providing more depth and complexity. And second, working with colour families will give you a large range to create enough contrast within your composition. Contrast is one of the most important aspects of colour. Simply put, it is the degree to which one colour is similar to another or different from it. Some colour combinations contrast dramatically, while others are much more subtle. More contrast is not necessarily better, but it's important to be aware that contrast in colour, and especially in lightness or darkness, will help you create dynamic compositions where even tiny stitches have presence.

Stitch directory

We think of stitches in a number of ways: an individual stitch is the smallest unit of embroidery, but stitches are also the result of a repeated action, technique and movement – a continuous collection. So knowing how to make a stitch is important, but knowing how to repeat and combine them is how we embroider. I mention this because stitches on their own can often be simple, but in combinations they can be quite complex. There are probably hundreds of stitches, from all cultures – maybe more. And no matter how you organize them into groups with similarities, variations and differences, the simple truth is there are a lot. And when we combine or embellish them, then even more.

Of course, as far as I'm concerned, there are no set rules about what should be used and where. But typically, most stitches are organized into a few categories based on appearance, use and intent. Outline stitches tend to be linear in nature, especially good for defining the edges of shapes, but also perfect for any design with linear elements. Border stitches are sometimes used simply to finish the fabric edges, but they are equally useful as decorative elements filling in open areas and framing areas of your design. Filler stitches provide dimension and solidity to shapes and forms, giving them character, colour and texture. A last category describes those that might be thought of as independent: little shapes or gestures that stand on their own. Now I won't try to provide you with a lengthy list, but here are some of my favourites that I return to again and again.

One note referring to the drawings and text: in many cases there are two ways to work your needle while embroidering. The first is 'stabbing' into your fabric, where the needle goes into the fabric completely to the back, before coming up completely out of the fabric at the front. Alternatively, 'sewing' is working the same stitch with the needle going in and out several times in one single action. Obviously this is faster, but is sometimes more difficult in tight fabric. How you work is up to you. For how to start your embroidery stitches see the quilter's knot on page 22, and to finish see the finishing knot on page 23.

Outline stitches

1.

2.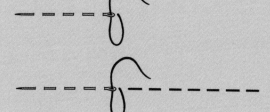

3.

1.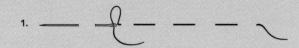

TACKING (BASTING) STITCH

When the stitches and spacing of running stitch becomes much longer (about 2.5cm/1in) then it is considered to be a tacking stitch, which is commonly used to temporarily hold together layers of fabric prior to permanent stitches. It can be used as a replacement for pins and is usually cut away after the final sewing is finished.

1. Follow the instructions for a running stitch but load your needle with fewer, longer stitches, and keep them rather loose so that they are easy to snip and remove.

RUNNING STITCH

A running stitch is one of the most common stitches used in all types of hand sewing and mending. In appearance it resembles a continuous line of little dashes. I usually try to keep the distance between stitches equal to the length of the actual stitches, but you may modify any spacing for visual impact. Loading the needle allows you to work faster than working one stitch at a time.

1. Pull the needle through the fabric from underneath until the knot hits the fabric.
2. Next, 'load' the stitches onto your needle, about three at a time depending on the length of the needle, in an under and over method, then pull the needle and thread through to get the resulting dashes.
3. Repeat as many times as necessary.

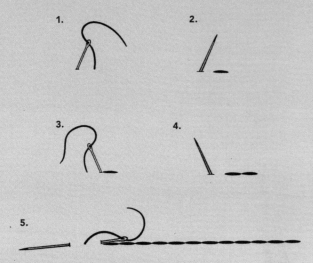

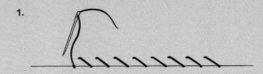

WHIP STITCH

A whip stitch is similar to a running stitch in that it is a continuous line of stitches with visible spaces between. But rather than appearing as a series of dashes in a single direction, they are stitched either on an angle or even perpendicular to the direction of the stitch line. Whip stitches can be used anywhere but are more commonly used along the edges where layers of fabric are sewn together, where two pieces of fabric are joined together, or where smaller pieces of fabric are sewn onto larger pieces.

1. Start your whip stitch underneath and bring the needle up through the fabric you wish to join. Make a stitch over the edge at the angle of your choice. Now, go underneath again to a position next to the previous stitch, then up through the fabric and over the edge. Repeat until the edges of the fabric are sewn together. The edges of the fabric can be rolled under to form a neat edge or left raw.

BACK STITCH

A back stitch is especially important for making imagery, or stitches that have the graphic quality of a line. It appears as a continuous line with tiny or no spaces in between the stitches, and is achieved by alternating in a forward and then backward direction.

1. Bring your needle up through the fabric from underneath to the front until your knot hits the underside of the fabric. Make one stitch in a forward direction.

2. With the needle now underneath again, continue in the same forward direction one equally spaced stitch ahead of the previous stitch, and bring the needle back through to the top.

3. Rather than continuing forward, now insert the needle back to the end of the last stitch, making the stitch line appear unbroken.

4. With the needle underneath and moving forward again, repeat these steps by bringing it back through to the top an equally spaced stitch beyond the last surface stitch, and then back again to join the last stitch.

5. Continuing with two spaces forward underneath, one space back on top, results in a continuous line of stitches.

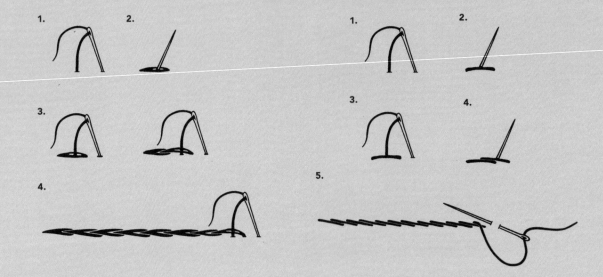

SPLIT STITCH

The split stitch is a basic embroidery stitch that can be used to outline an image or as a filler. It is very similar to a back stitch, but rather than going back to the end of the previous stitch from the top, you stab the previous stitch from below to create a continuous line. To use split stitch as a filler stitch, create an outline of the image then fill in with rows of stitches either next to each other or spaced slightly apart.

1. First determine your stitch length. Start by bringing the needle up from the back to the front and make a first stitch.
2. Now, with the needle underneath again, bring your needle up at a spot near the end, but within the previous stitch, thus splitting the threads of the previous stitch.
3. Then make your next stitch.
4. Repeat to make a line of stitches.

STEM STITCH

This stitch is a great one for outlining motifs as well as for linear elements. It has a nice shape and texture and gives the appearance of being somewhat organic; because it can be thicker than other stitches it is perfect for floral motifs such as stems.

1. Bring your needle up from the back and make the first stitch a bit longer than you normally would.
2. Then, with the needle underneath, come back up at the halfway point of the previous stitch, keeping on the stitch line but coming up just to one side.
3. Now go forward one stitch, again remembering to keep on the stitch line.
4. Then, from underneath, back up at the halfway point of the previous stitch.
5. Remember always to bring the needle up on the same side of the previous stitch to give the stitches a consistent look. Even though you are maintaining a single stitch line each stitch begins to one side of the previous stitch, which gives stem stitch a nice twisted look.

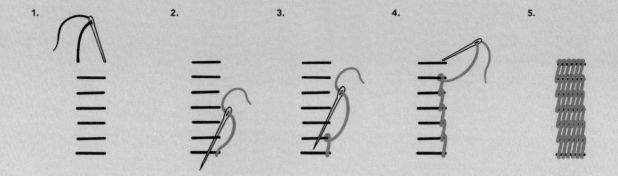

1.   2.   3.   4.   5.

RAISED STEM STITCH

A raised stem stitch has the appearance of a regular stem stitch, and is worked in a similar way, but rather than stitching into the base cloth you stitch into foundation stitches on the surface of the cloth. The raised stem stitch only enters the base cloth at the start and end of the shape that you are making, otherwise it lays on the surface. For one project I create a raised stem stitch on top of a rope (see page 117). This is done in the same manner, by creating a ladder of couching stitches first, then a series of raised stem stitches starting on one side and continuing back and forth until the couching is full and the rope is completely covered. The rope in this case creates a more 3D shape.

1. To start, create the foundation stitches. These are commonly couching (see page 39) or ladder stitches, worked to form a series of evenly spaced parallel lines across your shape.

2. You can create the raised stem stitch with a tapestry needle and a different colour thread, if you like. From below the first foundation line, come up and over to the second line.

3. Bring the needle over and around so that you wrap the working thread around the foundation stitch. Then take your needle over to the next line.

4. Wrap this line in the same manner, tightening your stitches as you proceed to the next line and so forth.

5. When you get to the last line, rather than wrapping around the line, go over it and back down into the cloth. At this point you can tie it off with a knot or go back underneath to start a new line of stitches next to the first. The shape, or band, is complete when the foundation stitches are full.

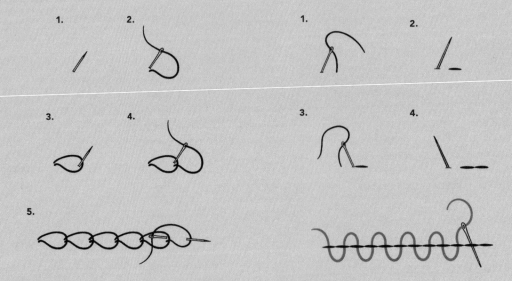

CHAIN STITCH

Chain stitch is one of the basic embroidery stitches that is useful for making a continuous line of conjoined loops like a chain. When layered beside each other it also makes a good filling stitch.

1. Starting from the back, bring the needle up at the beginning of the stitching line.

2. Insert your needle back down at the same point you came up, but don't pull it all the way through to the back. The working thread should form a small loop the length of your desired stitch.

3. Pointing the needle in the direction of the stitch line, bring the needle point up at a spot near the end of the loop but making sure to stay inside it. Pull gently to create the first stitch of the chain.

4. Repeat by making another loop the size of the first, and insert the needle back down into the same spot that you came up. Again, point the needle in the direction of the stitch line and up at a point near the end of the second loop. Gently pull, and repeat.

5. To finish a line of chain stitching, make a tiny stitch over the end of the last loop.

THREADED BACK STITCH

This is a variation on a back stitch that results from a combination of two stitches with contrasting colours. A back stitch line is laid down first and then a second thread is sewn within, without piercing the fabric. It maintains the linearity of back stitch but is fuller and more decorative, which is perfect for creating more elaborate lines and borders.

1. First, lay down a line of back stitch (see page 29). Thread your needle with a contrasting colour – since you will not be piercing the fabric you can use a blunt tapestry needle, which will make the threading easier.

2. Starting from the underside bring your needle up, coming out of the same hole where you started the back stitch.

3. Slide your needle under the first stitch of the back stitch, then, reversing direction, under the second stitch.

4. Repeat this along to create a line that zigzags back and forth along the back stitch.

5. You can pull the contrasting colour tight or leave loops each side. And, as another variation, you can weave an additional thread into the back stitch in the opposite direction with a third colour, resulting in loops on both sides.

BULLION STITCH

Bullion stitches are decorative stitches with wrapped threads, much like a French knot but elongated into a bar. They can be shaped into floral elements, or used to create texture. Because you wrap the thread around the needle it might be useful to use a longer needle such as a milliner's needle, which also has a small eye.

1. Bring your needle up from below at a point where you want your bullion stitch to start and bring it back down into the cloth where you want it to stop. You will use this distance to determine the number of wraps in the stitch. As you go back into the cloth do not pull the thread tight; instead leave a large loop of thread above.

2. Next, bring the needle up through the first hole but only about halfway out.

3. To create the knot, take the thread closest to the needle with one hand and wrap it around the needle, using your other hand to push the wraps down and steady the needle. You want the length of the wrapping on the needle to be the same as the distance between the two holes. Try not to wrap the thread too tightly or the next step of pulling the needle through the wrapping will be difficult.

4. Lightly pinch the wraps with one hand to hold them in place and pull the needle up and all the way through until the wrapping lays flat on the cloth.

5. Take the needle back down into the fabric through the second hole.

6. You'll have a neat line of wraps on the surface of the fabric. Repeat this to make more stitches or groups. If you want your bullion stitches to have more of a raised shape, make a shorter distance between the two holes and the length of the wrapping on the needle longer; when finished the stitch will naturally curve and form a shape.

1.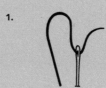

2.

3.

4.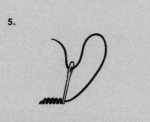

5.

6.

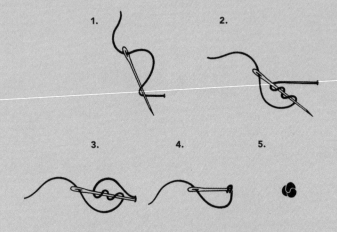

FRENCH KNOT

French knots are decorative stitches in the form of small, knotted dots. They can be used as filler, to make patterns or as the centres of floral motifs.

1. Bring your needle up where you would like your stitch to be.
2. Holding the needle in one hand, wrap the working thread around the shaft of the needle a couple of times or more, wrapping in the direction of the tip. The more times you wrap, the bigger the knot will be.
3. Continue to hold the thread that you wrapped in place and put the tip of the needle back into the cloth right next to the hole that you came out of. As you push the needle down, it's important to keep holding the wraps with your non-stitching hand.
4. Pull the needle down through the knot. As the loop gets smaller you can let the wraps go just before you pull the thread tight with the needle.
5. You'll end up with a neat knot on the surface of the fabric.

WHIPPED BACK STITCH

Whipped back stitches are perfect for linear elements but are more decorative than stitches with single lines. The back stitch acts as a foundation for the whip stitch so it seems somewhat raised, with a twisted appearance that can be accentuated with different colours of thread.

1. To start, create a line of back stitch (see page 29) to the desired length. To add the whip stitch, bring your needle up from the back at the beginning of the back stitch line.
2. Now wrap the thread around the back stitch by sliding the needle under each stitch in turn, without piercing the base cloth and always from the same direction. Continue for the entire length of back stitch.

TIP

This image shows how you can change the look of a piece through the line density by reducing or increasing the numbers of strands of threads (floss) you use when stitching.

Border stitches

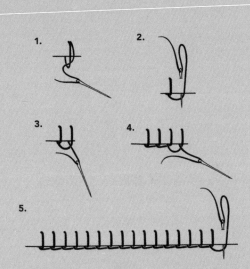

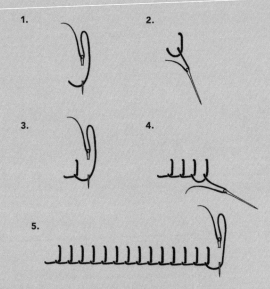

BLANKET STITCH WITH AN EDGE

This expressive stitch is typically used to create a finished, decorative edge. But blanket stitches are actually quite versatile; they can emphasize the edge of an opening or simply on their own as a surface stitch. In most cases blanket stitches maintain a consistent spacing and entry/exit points for the needle. I'm using 5mm (¼in), but feel free to establish your own spacing. If you are stitching along an edge the first stitch will be to anchor your thread.

1. Push the needle from the back through your fabric to the front, and about 5mm (¼in) or your desired spacing from the edge. Take the needle and thread around the edge and back up through the same hole that you started with to create a loop around the edge.
2. To finish the anchor, slide your needle sideways underneath the stitch you just made along the edge of the fabric.
3. To make your first blanket stitch, move your needle to a point 5mm (¼in) along to one side of your anchor stitch and 5mm (¼in) from the edge and take your needle to the back. Bring the tip up below the edge and pass it through the loop of the stitch.
4. Pull through and tighten.
5. Repeat this sequence along the edge.

BLANKET STITCH WITHOUT AN EDGE

If you are not stitching along an edge but onto the surface of your base cloth, the steps will be the same but usually without the need to start with a locking stitch.

1. Instead, tie a knot onto the end of your thread and come up from the back to begin. Then, moving your needle to a point 5mm (¼in) back and to the side, insert the needle through your fabric to the back, then out again along the same line that the first stitch started but 5mm (¼in) along.
2. Take the needle through the loop of the stitch, then tighten the loop.
3. The two lines, where your needle goes in and out, will establish the size of the stitches. You can change the spacing between stitches, the lengths of the vertical spokes, or make staggered lengths.
4. Repeat this sequence for each stitch.
5. To end your line of stitches, simply take your thread over the last loop and go back into the fabric to fasten off.

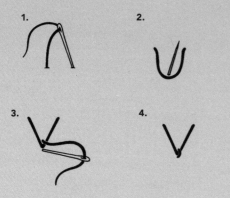

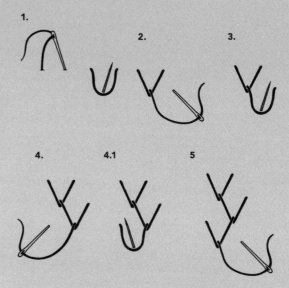

FLY STITCH

A fly stitch is a versatile stitch used to create shapes in the form of a 'V', 'U' or 'Y'. Singly, they can be used to make little shaped lines in your design and in groups they create little gestures that can be scattered about as a filler, or they can be lined up in rows to form borders – either alone or with other stitches. They are very simple to make and consist of two components: a horizontal stitch and a vertical.

1. To create the 'V' shape, come up from the back with your needle and thread and make a horizontal stitch, but don't tighten the thread yet – keep it loose like a small loop that hangs.
2. Now bring the needle up from the back at the midpoint where the point of a 'V' would be.
3. Wrap your thread around the loop and back into fabric to create a small vertical stitch that tacks the horizontal stitch down.
4. When you pull the thread taut it will form a 'V'. You can adjust the size and sharpness of the point by changing the location of the vertical stitch. A 'U' shape is made the same way but let your initial loop stay loose to form the 'U' shape rather than pulling it taut, as above. For the 'Y' shape, also called a long tail fly stitch, follow the steps for the 'V', but instead of a tiny stitch to tack down the loop make a longer vertical stitch. Then pull the thread taut to form the 'Y'.

FEATHER STITCH

This is a decorative stitch that is based on the fly stitch, but rather than making individual 'V' shapes you make vertical rows of continuous interlocked 'V' shapes. It makes lovely borders, especially when embellished with other stitches, but can also be a filler stitch when used in rows, or can even create even botanical elements with an organic feel.

1. Start by bringing the needle up from the back and make a horizontal stitch, keeping the thread in a loose loop.
2. Now, bring the needle up where the point of the 'V' would be, making sure to be just above the loop, not below.
3. Rather than make a vertical stitch as you would with the fly stitch, make another horizontal stitch to one side (doesn't matter which side), again leaving the stitch loose like a loop.
4. Bring the needle back up above the loop. The second stitch now appears as one 'V' beneath the other and slightly offset.
5. Make another horizontal stitch, this time in the opposite direction. Continue this repetition and you will create a row of 'V' shapes, alternating from one side to the other.

Filler stitches

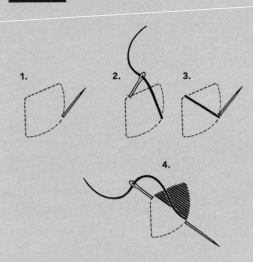

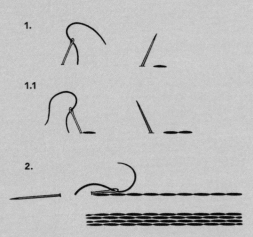

SATIN STITCH

A satin stitch is one of the most common filler stitches, which can be used to fill in any shape with an area of flat, smooth and closely spaced stitches. Each stitch lays parallel to the last, extending across the entire length or width of the shape.

1. Begin by lightly drawing or stitching the outline of the shape on the fabric. I prefer starting at one end at the narrowest point of the shape, but others start stitching at the midway point to help keep the stitches parallel.

2. Bring the threaded needle up from the back, making sure to start at the outside of your line and make the first stitch across and down again on the other side of the shape.

3. Take the next stitch right next to the first, using your drawing to determine the length of the stitch.

4. Repeat, making each stitch longer or shorter as necessary. You are aiming to fill the shape with solid colour. Try to make each stitch lay flat next to each other and avoid too much overlapping. Take care that you don't pull the stitches too tight or it will pull the fabric and cause puckering.

BRICK STITCH

Like satin stitch, this is a simple filler stitch that uses parallel stitches placed tightly next to each other. But, rather than single stitches that span the entire length of a shape, brick stitch uses a combination of short and long stitches that create a brick-like pattern. The combination of stitch lengths gives it more texture, and opportunities to combine different colours and gradations into the pattern.

1. Start by laying down a line of back stitch (see page 29) , maintaining a consistent length of stitch.

2. Now, right next to where you started, make another line of back stitch but make the first one only half as long, so it ends at the halfway point of the stitch next to it. Continue with stitches the same size as in the first line, with each stitch ending at the midway point of the stitch beside it. Continue row by row, alternating the size of the stitches at the start and end to create the staggered brick pattern.

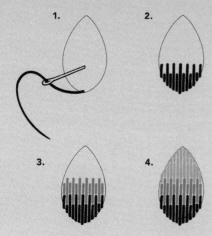

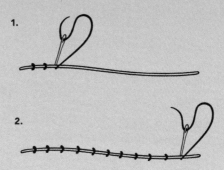

LONG AND SHORT STITCH

Long and short stitches are used when blending colours and creating gradations with a series of intermingled stitches of various sizes. The resulting gradations not only provide depth of colour but can emphasize shape and dimensions. On larger areas it is sometimes useful to begin by drawing direction lines on the cloth in pencil to help you keep your stitches straight. Determine the gradation by choosing the number of colours or tones – if using three colours, your shape should have three zones, each blending into the next.

1. With the first colour in the first zone, start stitching using different lengths of stitches, trying to be a little random and inconsistent.

2. Continue until you have finished the first zone.

3. Once you have finished this zone go to the next colour – now you will fade the two colours together by interlocking long stitches with short stitches. You can try and skip around so that it keeps the stitch length inconsistent.

4. When you have completed all the colours you will have achieved a lovely graded effect.

COUCHING

This technique uses two threads, one that is laid down on the surface and one that is stitched over it to hold it down. You can use two different colour threads, or two the same colour.

1. Bring the first thread up through the fabric and lay it along the surface in whatever shape or line you wish. Thread a second needle and bring it up through the fabric just below the line of the laid thread, wrap around it with a tiny vertical whip stitch over the top and go back down into the base cloth near to where you came out. In essence, you are creating a stitch perpendicular to the laid thread to hold it down. After this first stitch, move along a little and repeat.

2. Continue along the laid thread until it is held down with stitches along its entire length. To finish the line, take the laid thread and, underneath, turn it around to run back on top of itself for a length equal to a few stitches. Continue making small whip stitches in the second thread to fasten the folded end to the base cloth. Tie the second thread from below to end the line of stitches.

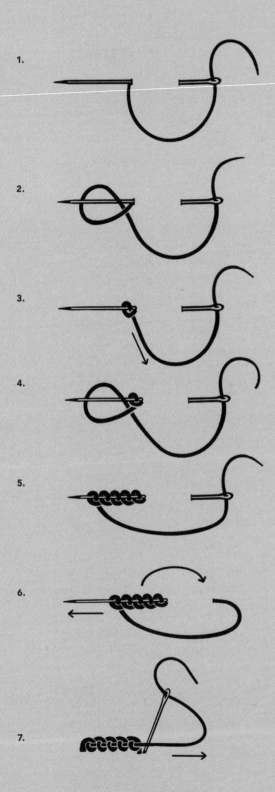

CAST ON STITCH

The cast on stitch is a type of dimensional or raised embroidery that appears as a little arch of stitches attached to the base cloth at either end, but free and raised above the base cloth in the middle. It can be a shallow arch or a high loop, depending on how you start. It can be used where you want raised areas of texture and can also make lovely little spirals and 3D flowers.

1. Bring your needle up through the fabric, take a stitch back and put it back into the fabric, bringing the tip out at the point you started. Don't pull the needle out, leave it sitting in the fabric at both points. The distance between the two points will, in part, determine the shape of the cast on stitch. If it is similar to the length of exposed needle point, then your stitch will sit flatter, if it is shorter than the length of exposed needle point, it will sit higher as a loop.

2. Now cast on a series of stitches onto the tip of the needle, in the form of a row of twisted loops wrapped around the needle, one at a time. Take your working thread and place it over your finger, while you hold it somewhat taut with your other hand. Twist your finger to create a loop, with the thread closest to the needle over top of the thread in your hand. Slip the loop onto the needle tip.

3. Pull gently on the working thread to bring the stitch close to the fabric and tighten the stitch.

4. Repeat this step, casting on stitches one by one, tightening them as you go.

5. You want to create a length of stitches at least as long as the length of the needle underneath the base cloth. Casting on more stitches will make a loop that sits higher off the fabric.

6. Next, hold onto the stitches between your fingers with one hand and gently pull the needle through and completely out of the cast on stitches. Continue to pull the needle and thread, coaxing the stitch over towards the other stitch point. Pull the thread until the cast on stitches sit tight to the base cloth.

7. Lastly, take the loose thread and take it back into the cloth near to the end of the stitch to fix it to the base cloth.

WEAVE STITCH

Over/under weaving techniques are common elements in different types of embroidery stitches, but on its own this is a simple and fast way of creating filler stitches. Like most simple stitches, there are also plenty of ways to make it visibly complex by mixing thread types, varying your spacing, and playing with colour and tone. By adjusting these variables you can create all sorts of textures, patterns and shading.

1. Create your foundation stitches by filling in the shape with parallel stitches, usually vertical at first, that start at one edge and span the entire height of your shape to the other edge. In weaving terms this would be the warp.

2. To keep the back free from long strands, start your stitch by coming up from below, go across the shape, then into your fabric on the other side. Now, underneath the edge, slide over by however wide you want your spacing to be and bring the needle up from the back.

3. Then repeat, going back and forth until the shape is filled.

4. Now, create a series of parallel stitches in the same manner, but in a horizontal direction. In weaving this would be the weft. You may want to switch to a tapestry needle with a blunter point to aid the weaving. Starting from below, bring your needle up and pass over the first of the vertical foundation stitches, then continue by alternating under, over, under, weaving across all the vertical stitches until you reach the other side of the shape. As with the vertical stitches, take your needle to the back of your fabric, then slide to the side the distance you want for your spacing, and come up to begin to weave in the other direction. Alternate the over/under of the previous row – if one stitch is over/under, the next will be under/over.

5. As you weave each row, push with your needle to straighten the previous row so that everything is neat and spaced as you like.

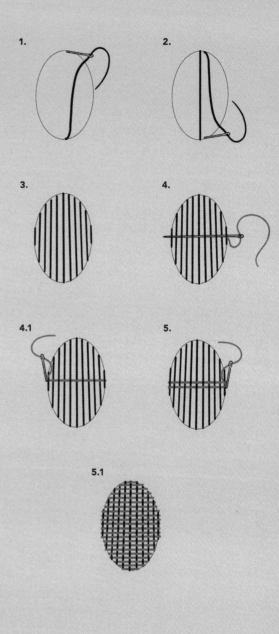

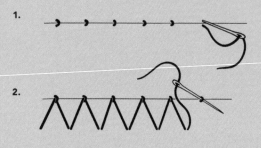

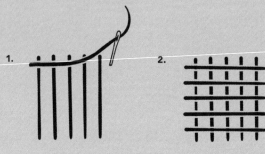

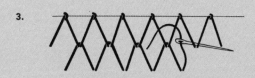

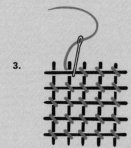

WAVE STITCH

I enjoy doing this stitch when the rows are slightly uneven, and it gives the final shape a nice organic movement.

1. Start by creating a row of small vertical stitches.
2. Bring your needle up from the back just one stitch to the left and below the small stitches. Insert the needle under the small stitch and pull it through and back down to create an inverted 'V'. Keep repeating this until all the small stitches have been sewn under.
3. For the next row bring your needle from the back a stitch length underneath the centre of the inverted 'V' above, and then take your needle through the bottom of that stitch at its foot.

JACOBEAN COUCHING/TRELLIS

This stitch is a quick way to cover large areas with a horizontal and vertical grid of thread, where the base cloth is still visible between the threads. With the addition of small stitches to hold everything down, different colours can make this type of embroidery quite decorative. It works best with heavier threads, or even yarns.

1. To begin, create either the horizontal or vertical lines of thread with each line parallel and spaced equally – it's up to you to determine the spacing. Start by coming up from beneath and make one long stitch from one edge to the other, spanning the entire shape. Continue, making long stitches to evenly cover the entire shape.
2. Next, cover the shape with evenly spaced threads perpendicular to the first stitches. It is not necessary to weave the threads over and under, simply place this layer of stitches on top of the first layer.
3. Lastly, make diagonal couching stitches (see page 39) to hold the thread down where the horizontal and vertical threads intersect. These can be small single seed stitches (see page 45). Make sure that they all go in the same direction, or if you like you can create little cross stitches. Using a different colour for the couching stitches makes them stand out from the grid.

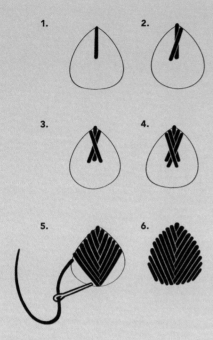

FISHBONE STITCH

This stitch is perfect to create a slightly raised leaf design, so draw a suitable leaf shape on your fabric first.

1. Come up from the back at the top of the leaf and go down the centre with a long stitch length.

2. Then bring your needle up at the top again and on the right-hand side of the first stitch and go down just below and over the first stitch you created.

3. Then go to the left side of the centre stitch at the top and come down to the bottom of it, again over the top.

4. Keep coming up along the outline, first on one side and then on the other, and going down below the stitches in the centre, creating a slight overlap each time.

5. Keep going until you have filled the centre of the leaf.

6. Make small individual stitches on each side to fill in the base of the leaf if necessary.

43

Independent stitches

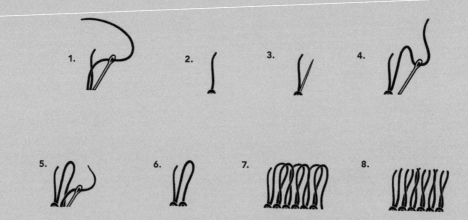

TURKEY WORK/FRINGE

Turkey work creates a plush pile of looped stitches on the surface of your work – it consists of a series of loops each tied down with a small locking stitch. The name is derived from a technique common in the country of Turkey. You might think of it as a raised stitch because the loops can be made as high as you like, or you can snip the loops to create a fringe or tufts. Typically, you create a single line of stitches, either straight or curved, to make a fringe, but to fill an area you make a number of parallel stitching lines. The end result can be a little unruly, but you can tame it with a few strokes from your needle.

1. Start by going into the fabric from the front, leaving a tail with no knot at whatever length you want the loops to be. Now, create a small stitch that will lock the tail in place by coming back up just to the left of the tail and going down just to the right of it.

2. Tighten the small stitch to secure the tail.

3. Next come up from the bottom at the same location as the tail and pull your thread all the way through.

4. At this point you will create your first loop, so go forward a stitch length and back into the fabric, pulling your thread through, but leaving a loop the size you want.

5. Create the locking stitch by coming back up just to the left of the loop and going back down just to the right, then tighten the stitch.

6. Continue to make your loops, each finished with a locking stitch.

7. For a loose pile make the loops beside each other, for a denser pile make them overlap each other.

8. You can leave the Turkey work as a pile of loops, or you can cut the tops off to create tufts.

SEED STITCH

A seed stitch consists of simple little stitches used to fill an area. Some see the seed stitch as a variation of a running stitch, sharing a direction but with smaller stitches on top of the fabric. I prefer to define it as small stitches that fill an area more randomly, all similar in size, but pointing in any direction so that it appears organic.

1. Start by bringing your needle up from the back and make a short stitch anywhere on the cloth, then take your needle back down. Repeat this, with each stitch oriented in a slightly different direction so there is no overall pattern. Try to keep each stitch similar in length, and more or less equally spaced, scattered over the base cloth. As a variation, you can work seed stitches into clusters, with differing amounts of space between.

EYELET

An eyelet is a small hole in the fabric that is finished around the edge with some form of decorative stitching.

1. First create a small hole in the fabric where you want the eyelet to be. You can also mark your circular stitching line around it as a guide.
2. Bring the needle through from the back along your stitching line, and go down into the centre hole.
3. Keep repeating this step, keeping the stitches close together.
4. Fasten off when you have edged the circle all the way around. You can experiment and try different embroidery stitches around the edge.

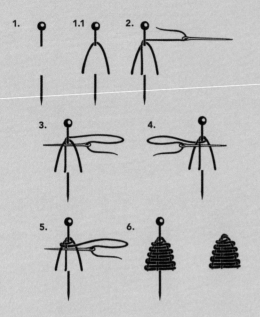

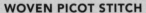

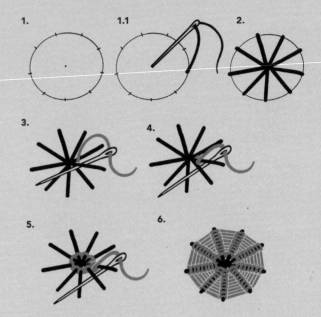

WOVEN PICOT STITCH

This stitch creates a 3D petal or leaf-like shape with a lovely texture.

1. First put a long straight pin in the fabric to the height you want your picot stitch to be. Bring the thread up from the back on the left side and wrap it behind the pin, then take it down to the right of the pin. Make sure the distance on both sides is equal from the pin in the centre.

2. Come up next to the pin at bottom left and pass this thread to the back of the head of the pin.

3. At the top you will start creating your weave pattern by going under and over the three strands of thread.

4. Weave the rest of the shape by alternating under and over the threads, working from left to right and right to left.

5. Every so often push up the rows so that they are not loose and will fit snugly together. When you have filled in the picot you can take the needle down toward the base of the shape and create a finishing knot at the back.

6. Pull the pin out and you will have a nice shape that you can move, but which is anchored at the base. If you like you can also anchor the top of the shape down by adding a small stitch at the top. Experiment with how many threads you use to make the shape wider or narrower.

RIBBED SPIDER STITCH

This creates a round shape with spokes that are wrapped, which accentuates them more than in Woven Spider's Web/Wheel.

1. Start by drawing a circle the size you want and marking the spokes around the edge – it doesn't matter if you have an even or an odd number of spokes. Come up from the back and down to the centre to stitch the first spoke.

2. Repeat to stitch all the spokes of your wheel.

3. Next bring the working thread up from the centre – for this you might want to use a different colour. To make it easier at this point I would also switch to a tapestry needle, or if you don't have one you can use the eye side of your needle. Start by going underneath the first spoke.

4. Go back around that same spoke and then go forward under the next spoke.

5. Keep going, wrapping each spoke in turn, then work the next round. As you go around the circle, pack in your stitches without overlapping them.

6. Keep repeating these steps until all of the circle is filled up. Finish by taking the needle down under the last spoke, pull through and create a finishing knot (see page 23).

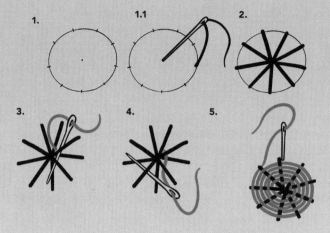

WOVEN SPIDER'S WEB/WHEEL

This is similar to Ribbed Spider Stitch but you weave under and over the spokes in a spiral, so they are not so prominent in the finished stitch.

1. Start by drawing a circle the size you want and marking the spokes around the edge – for this stitch it must be an odd number of spokes, and Start from the outside edge and go back down into the centre to create the first spoke.

2. Repeat to stitch all the spokes of your wheel.

3. Next bring the working thread up from the centre – for this you might want to use a different colour and switch to a tapestry needle. Start by going under the first stitch and over the next one.

4. Repeat this around the centre, going under and over each spoke in turn.

5. On the next round you will alternate, so if you went under on one round you will go over on the next one. As you get closer to the outside of the shape try to make sure the threads remain flat. When you are done pull the thread to the back and tie a finishing knot (see page 23).

Home

Patchwork lavender sachet

———

This project is for a little lavender sachet, but it can also be made as a pincushion. It doesn't require anything new: you can use the remnants from other projects. The patchwork is quick and easy enough to make several, all with different colours or patterns. While the embroidery for this is a simple abstract set of diagonal lines, it can easily be modified with your own design or you can use one of the images from the Woodland Badges or Pins (see page 71) or Mini Hoop Pendants (see page 75) projects.

Skill level: Easy

YOU WILL NEED

Selection of coloured linen remnants or
    0.25m (¼yd) medium-weight fabric
2 pieces of linen fabric per sachet in a light
    natural colour, each 12.5cm (5in) square
Scissors and snips
Sewing machine – optional
Sewing needles and thread
Iron
Pencil or washable marker
13cm (5in) embroidery hoop (If you don't have
    a small hoop you can hold the fabric
    in your hand to embroider)
DMC thread (floss) in:
    Sachet 1 – gold (676), dark red (3777)
    Sachet 2 – coral (350), pink (3779)
    Sachet 3 – dark grey (3799), dark yellow (3820)
No. 5 or 6 embroidery needle
Dried lavender or wool fleece stuffing

Instructions

——

1. This project is a little different than others in that the sewing is all done first, then the embroidery afterwards. Cut the coloured linen into strips 4cm (1½in) wide, then into pieces – you'll need four 7.5 x 4cm (3 x 1½in) strips and four 4cm (1½in) squares in a contrast colour for each sachet. Cut one piece of the natural-colour linen down to a 7.5cm (3in) square. On one side of this square sew a strip of 7.5 x 4cm (3 x 1½in) coloured linen. Sew this strip on as you would joining pieces of a patchwork quilt, by laying the strip right sides together on top of the square, aligned on one edge, and sewing along the edge with a 1cm (⅜in) seam allowance. Then repeat with a same colour strip on the opposite side of the square. Put aside for a moment.

2. Make up two more strips, both consisting of a 7.5 x 4cm (3 x 1½in) piece of coloured fabric with a 4cm (1½in) square of contrast fabric on both ends. Sew in the same manner as in step 1, with a 1cm (⅜in) seam allowance.

3. Now, take the piece made up in step 1 and sew one strip from step 2 onto the other two sides so that you now have a natural linen square with strips of colour on all sides and contrasting corners. Again, sew as above with a 1cm (⅜in) seam allowance. When you have finished the sewing, press all the seams flat with an iron. Cut the other piece of natural-colour linen down to the same dimensions as your finished patchwork, for the back.

4. Draw some simple diagonal lines freehand onto the middle square, and on the squares next to it around the edge of the patchwork. The outside squares have spaces between each line, the centre square has no spaces so it will appear as a solid square of colour when stitched. You can also come up with your own design instead.

5. Fix the fabric in the hoop. If you don't have a small hoop you can hold the fabric in your hand to embroider. Embroider the lines using stem stitch (see page 30 for stitch instructions), using the first colour for the middle square and the second colour for the outside squares. The direction of the diagonal stitching is not important, but a variety makes for a nice organic look. Once you finish the embroidery design, remove the hoop and press the fabric one more time (see page 21).

6. Place the back piece with right sides facing on top of the patch piece. Sew around the perimeter with a 1cm (⅜in) seam allowance, leaving an unsewn gap of around 5cm (2in) along one side.

7. Clip the corners and turn right side out. Press flat with an iron. Pour dried lavender inside the sachet (at this point if you want to make a pin cushion you can use the wool fleece to fill it instead) and hand sew the opening closed with a blind stitch (see page 23) or whip stitch (see page 29).

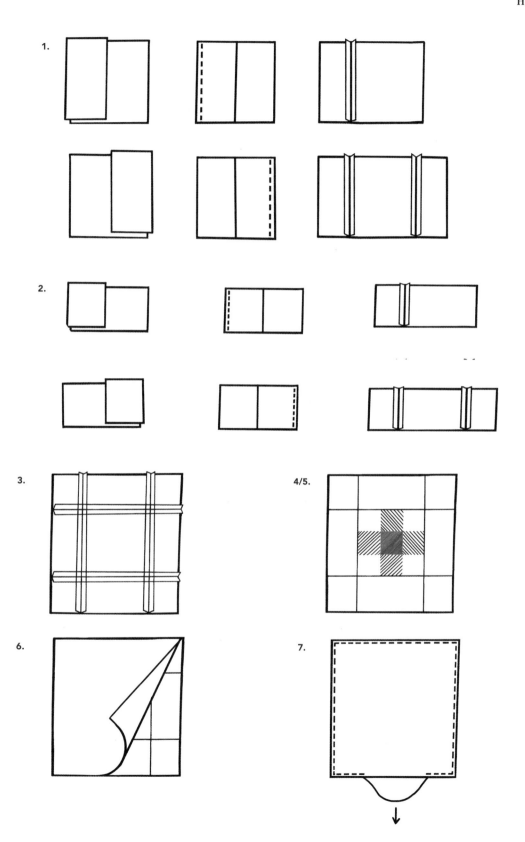

1.

2.

3.

4/5.

6.

7.

Appliqué poppy cushion

—

I love creating surface design on cushions using a variety of elements because it's like making small works of art. Combinations of layers and materials, colour and textures can add so much visual interest to an otherwise everyday object. For this one I have chosen wool fabric in three tones of warm pink. Because the edges of wool don't fray, it gives the shapes a nice clean edge that really complements the black lines of the embroidery.

Skill level: Easy

YOU WILL NEED

58.5cm (23in) square of ivory linen fabric

Pencil or heat-erasable pen

15cm (6in) square of Wonderfil wool fabric in each of salmon, primrose and rhubarb

Scissors and snips

25cm (10in) no-slip hoop

8 skeins of DMC thread (floss) in black (310)

No. 3 or 4 embroidery needle

Appliqué pins or safety pins

Overlocker (serger) – optional

Sewing machine with zipper foot and thread

Iron

Ruler or tape measure

48.25cm (19in) square of ivory linen fabric

35cm (14in) ivory plastic zipper

45cm (18in) square cushion pad (pillow form)

TIPS

The larger piece of linen fabric size includes extra fabric to allow it to fit in the hoop. The smaller piece includes a 1cm (⅜in) seam allowance all round.

You could just work the embroidery on a plain ready-made cover if you don't want to make up your own cover.

Wonderfil Merino wool fabric is sold in packs with a selection of colours – the 'orange' pack includes the colours you will need for this project.

Instructions

——

1. Download and print the templates from www. bookhou.com/pages/embroidery-patterns to 43cm (17in) wide. Place the template right in the middle on top of the 58.5cm (23in) square of linen and trace the pattern using a pencil or heat-erasable pen (see page 18 for transfer techniques). For the time being, only trace the stem and leaves as well as the overall cushion shape. For the round flower appliqué area it may be easier if you cut out the round flower shapes from the printed template and use them as a pattern to cut out the felt shapes. This will give you a bit of freedom with the flower placement and it will also be easier not to have the wool flowers pinned in place when stretching the linen on your hoop. Stretch the fabric in your hoop (see page 21 for stretching instructions).

2. Make up an arm's length of 8 strands of black embroidery thread and thread onto a needle size 3 or 4. Tie a quilter's knot (see page 22) at the end and begin by coming up from underneath. The embroidery for the entire piece was done in a stem stitch (see page 30 for stitch instructions). Begin the embroidery work on the linen cloth following your drawn out pattern of the leaves and stems. I tend to work from left to right and bottom to the top, but choose whatever direction suits you best.

3. Once the embroidery for all the leaves and stems is completed, pin the wool appliqué flowers in place using appliqué pins or safety pins. Next, using the heat-erasable pen or pencil, draw lines on the wool fabric starting in the middle and branching out to the edge, keeping the lines about 5mm (¼in) apart at their widest, but it's fine if you want fewer lines with more space in between. Embroider a stem stitch along the drawn lines, moving the pins as you work. I worked from the edge to the middle but you can do the opposite if you like. Try to keep your appliqué flat and be mindful of your

tension, so not to cause the fabric to pucker. Continue this way until all the flowers are stitched and the appliqué pieces are attached. After you're done you can give the area a press with the iron.

4. The next step is to sew the pillow. To start, trim the embroidered front to 48.25cm (19in) square and overlock (serge) the edges of the front and back so that they do not fray. If you don't have a overlocker you can do a zigzag or straight stitch on the sewing machine instead. Placing the back on top of the front with right sides facing each other and sew the bottom edges together with a 1cm (⅜in) seam at the right and left corners for about 6cm (2½in), leaving a large gap in between for the zipper. Flatten the seam with an iron, including the unsewn gap for the zipper. This will help to keep your lines straight when sewing the zipper.

5. Open the cushion sides out with the right sides facing up. Place the zipper underneath centred within the unsewn gap and sew the zipper to the two sides using a zipper foot. Make sure to sew all four sides of the zipper. Open the zipper and fold the cushion so that the right sides are once again facing each other and sew along the other three side of the cuahion with a 1cm (⅜in) seam allowance. Once you are done sewing, turn the pillow with right side out, press the fabric and place the cushion pad (pillow form) inside.

4.

4.1.

4.2.

5.

5.1.

5.2.

5.3.

Meadow napkin

———

Embroidering on napkins gives your dining table a lovely personalized look, especially when using vintage napkins or fabric. These would also make great housewarming gifts. I chose a floral motif and placed it on the corner, so that when the napkins are folded next to the place setting they show off the embroidery work.

Skill level: Easy

YOU WILL NEED

Set of 43cm (17in) square vintage napkins, or fabric to make new ones

Sewing machine and thread, if making your own napkins

Sulky Stick 'n Stitch

25cm (10in) hoop

Sajou Retors du Nord thread (floss) in Salmon (2036), Moss (2034), Boxwood (2023)

DMC thread (floss) in dark green (934), light gold (422)

No. 7–10 embroidery needle

Scissors and snips

Iron

Instructions

––––

1. I created my own napkins by cutting 4 pieces of fabric each 46cm (18in) square and sewing a 5mm (¼in) rolled hem all around the edges. Download and print the templates from www.bookhou.com/pages/embroidery-patterns onto the Stick 'n Stitch at the size you want, and cut away any extra paper so that you are left with just the image with a small border. Peel and place where you want the image to be – I folded the napkin first to get the design in the right position in one corner.

2. Stretch the fabric over a hoop (see page 21 for stretching instructions) and start by stitching the stem in dark green. I mostly used satin stitch or short and long stitch for the flowers (see pages 38 and 39 for stitch instructions). Because the Stick 'n Stitch material is between the cloth and the threads it's good to go a bit tighter with your stitches so that you don't have any loose threads.

3. After you finish the stem, stitch the flower petals in light gold. I tried to make sure there were gaps left in between the petals so they looked like individual shapes. I then stitched the leaves on the stem in Salmon and the ones on the flower stem in Moss and Boxwood.

4. When you have finished all the embroidery wash away the Stick 'n Stitch – it will dissolve under water – lay the napkin to dry and then press with an iron if needed.

1.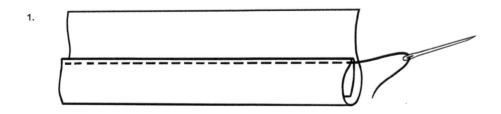

Wool flower cushion

―――――

Shaped cushions always make nice accent decorations and this one can fit into any situation with its minimal palette. But you can definitely adapt this design for a square cushion or even stitch onto an existing fabric pillow. For this design I kept it monochromatic and used wool threads to give the surface some texture.

Skill level: Easy

YOU WILL NEED

20 skeins of Appleton crewel thread in cream (992)

2 pieces of dark grey linen fabric, each approx. 50cm (20in) square

Pins

Graphite transfer paper

Pencil

Heat-erasable pen (optional)

25cm (10in) no-slip hoop

No. 7 embroidery needle

Scissors and snips

Sewing machine and thread

Polyester fibre filler or 46cm (18in) diameter cushion pad (pillow form)

Instructions

—

1. Download and print the templates from www.
   bookhou.com/pages/embroidery-patterns
   to 33cm (13in) square for an 46cm (18in)
   diameter cushion. Place the template in the
   middle on the right side of one of the linen
   pieces and pin in place. Because the fabric
   I used was dark I found the best method to
   transfer was to put graphite transfer paper
   underneath the image, facing down and to
   trace directly onto the cloth, lifting the linen
   up now and then to see how the transferring
   was progressing (see page 18 for transfer
   techniques). If there are areas that are not
   visible go over that area freehand with
   a heat-erasable pen to darken the pattern,
   using the template as a reference.

2. Choose a section and stretch the linen
   onto your hoop (see page 21 for stretching
   instructions). Thread an arm's length of
   thread onto a no. 7 embroidery needle and
   tie a quilter's knot (see page 22) at the end.

3. See pages 27–47 for all embroidery stitch
   instructions. I used chain stitch to create the
   outline and fill in the more solid areas. Begin
   embroidering and complete the area within
   the hoop before restretching and moving
   to the next area. Work on the outlines first
   before filling in any solid elements.

4. When the embroidery is complete add about
   7.5cm (3in) all around the design, which
   includes a 1cm (⅜in) seam allowance all
   around, and trim the fabric down. Trim the
   second piece of linen to the same size for
   the back of the cushion.

5. Place the front and the back with the right sides
   facing each other. Sew around the edge with
   a 1cm (⅜in) seam allowance, leaving a 10cm
   (4in) unsewn gap along the bottom. Make
   small snips into the seam allowance all around
   the cushion so that the edge will have a nice
   curve when right side out. When finished, turn
   the cover right side out by pulling through the
   unsewn gap.

6. Stuff the inside of the cushion with filler or
   a cushion pad, and sew the gap closed using
   small blind stitches (see page 23) or whip
   stitches (see page 29) and trying to keep
   them as invisible as possible.

4.

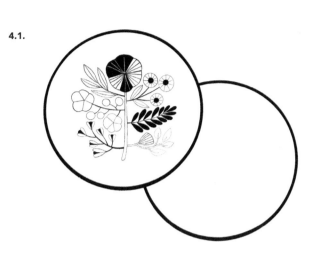

4.1.

5.

5.1.

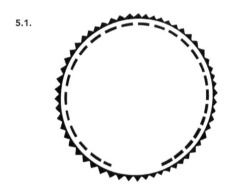

5.2

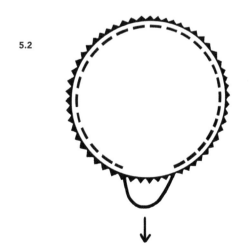

6.

Woodland badges or pins

———

Everyone who works with fabric in any way has plenty of leftovers and remnants, usually tucked away waiting for the perfect reason to go through them. Well, here are some projects that are not only perfect for whatever you have to hand, but are also a great way to practise your embroidery skills. I have a button machine that I use for these, but a button cover kit is equally good if you remove the loop on the back and glue a pin back to it instead. You can also find other types of pin holder online that might work, too. I like making these as a last-minute gift that I can pin onto decorated card stock.

Skill level: Easy

YOU WILL NEED

Button cover kit or badge-making machine

Remnant fabric in a variety of cottons or linens in any colour

Pencil or water-soluble pen

Sulky Stick 'n Stitch – optional for dark fabrics

Scissors and snips

18cm (7in) embroidery hoop

DMC thread (floss) in:

Apple – deep red (817), dark blue-green (319)

Ladybird – black (310), deep red (817)

Sprigs – dark blue-green (319), golden brown (420)

Bee – straw yellow (3821), black (310)

Cat – dark grey (3799)

Bird – dark grey (3799), dark gold (3852), sage green (522)

Daisy flower – straw yellow (3821), pale gold (677), red-brown (918)

Tulip flower with stem – mauve (316), pine green (3364), topaz (780)

Round flower with stem – red-brown (918), pale terracotta (3778), avocado green (471), yellow-green (3819)

Butterfly – dark grey (3799), dark gold (3852), topaz (780), mauve (316)

Moth – topaz (780), turquoise (3845), deep red (817), dark blue-green (319), pale gold (677), Ecru

No. 5 or 6 embroidery needle

Interfacing – optional

Instructions

―――――

1. To start, make a template sized for the badge or button cover that you are using, so that you know how big to make your image – if you make it too big, its edges might get cropped. Make sure that you leave a seam allowance of 3mm (⅛in) all the way around for the edge that gets tucked under. Stretch your fabric onto your hoop if it is large enough, if it is not you can hold it in your hand to embroider. Trace the circles onto the pieces of cloth you are using. Feel free to draw as many circles next to each other as you like.

2. Download and print the template www. bookhou.com/pages/embroidery-patterns onto paper, or Stick 'n Stitch if you are using a darker fabric, sized for your circles. Transfer the images onto your fabric (see page 18 for transfer techniques), centred in the circles. If your fabric is lightweight you can trace the images using a pencil over a photocopy against a window.

3. For the majority of the images I used satin stitch and French knots, see pages 27–47 for all embroidery stitch instructions. If you like, you can use other stitches instead, such as back stitch or stem stitch for outlining the shapes.

4. When you have finished all the embroidery on your piece of fabric, cut the circles out, again remembering to add a little room all around for the fabric that gets tucked under the button edges. Then, follow the badge-making machine or button cover tool instructions to finish, adding a layer of interfacing under the embroidered fabric if necessary.

TIPS

It's a good idea to put interfacing under your fabric if it's lightweight – this will reduce the shine of the metal button from showing through.

If the fabric pieces are too small for a hoop you can just hold them in your hand to embroider.

Mini hoop pendants

———

This mini hoop pendant is another great way to use up some of your remnant fabrics and create a small-scale work of art that is wearable. There are a lot of mini hoops on the market and I found some that were made from hardwood and have a really lovely finish. They come in different shapes and sizes, and you can add a chain or ribbon to make it perfect to wear as a pendant or glue on a pin back and wear it as a brooch.

Skill level: Easy

YOU WILL NEED

Remnants of linen fabric in a variety of colours, sized larger than your mini hoop

Graphite transfer paper

Pencil or heat-erasable pen (optional)

Mini wood hoop

Scissors and snips

Embroidery hoop – optional

DMC thread (floss) in black (310), pale terracotta (3778), olive green (733), dark green (934), dark yellow (3820), chocolate brown (975), dark gold (3852), deep pink (335), lime green (166), moss green (581), grey (535)

Sajou Retors du Nord thread (floss) in Coral (2017), Nankin (2038), Nile (2449), Emerald (2777), Autumn (2549), Navy (2864)

No. 5 or 6 embroidery needle

White craft glue

TIPS

You can find mini wood hoops online; I used ones from Artbase, which are made of hardwood.

If the pieces are too small to embroider in a hoop, you can just hold the fabric in your hand.

Instructions

1. Download and print the templates from www.bookhou.com/pages/embroidery-patterns to fit your mini hoop, remembering to add at least 2cm (¾in) all around to stretch the fabric around the base of the mini hoop. Since most of the coloured linen that I used is hard to see through, I printed the image out at the appropriate size and used graphite transfer paper (see page 18 for transfer techniques). If you want to draw directly on the fabric freehand, you can simply refer to the template images and use a pencil or a heat-erasable pen. It may also be helpful to draw the overall hoop shape by tracing the inside ring and adding the seam allowance so you know where to cut out upon completion.

2. If your fabric is large enough you can draw or transfer several images and stretch the fabric on an embroidery hoop, moving the fabric as you work. If you are using small bits of fabric that are too small for a hoop, I sometimes find it easier to just hold them in my hand without stretching. It won't be possible to stitch directly in the mini hoops as the ones I used have a solid backing insert that is used to mount your image.

3. Start your embroidery by referring to the stitch diagram and see pages 27–47 for stitch instructions. Most of the stitches I used were satin or back stitches, with the occasional French knot in flower centres for variety and texture. This project is completely open-ended, though, so feel free to interpret the images with your own thoughts about stitches or colours.

4. When you have finished your stitching, cut the image out, including the seam allowance, and mount it into the mini hoop according to the hoop instructions. To finish the back, thread a needle leaving the end unknotted. Sew a running stitch around the edge, just inside the frame. When done, tie the two ends together and pull the thread taut, cinching the selvedge together.

5. The hoops I used came with a backing, so add some glue to the wood back and place it on the back of the mini hoop. Add a chain or ribbon to make a pendant, or glue a pin back to the back for a brooch.

Daisy purse

————

There is something about purse frames that make a project seem so finished and special. They come in many different sizes and shapes with so many options and varieties – there are even ones that you can sew the fabric onto. And, of course, they're incredibly useful. The pattern and instructions are for a 10 x 5cm (4 x 2in) metal purse frame. They may not be suitable for a differently sized or shaped purse frame, but there are lots of resources you can find online to help you create custom patterns.

Skill level: Advanced

YOU WILL NEED

2 pieces of linen fabric, each approx. 25cm (10in) square
Pencil
18cm (7in) embroidery hoop
Sajou Retours du Nord thread (floss) in Warbler (2016), Flesh (2348), Army Green (2615)
DMC thread (floss) in dark yellow (3820)
No. 7 milliner's needle
No. 5 or 6 embroidery needle
2 pieces of lining fabric, each approx. 20cm (8in) square
Scissors and snips
Iron
10 x 5cm (4 x 2in) metal purse frame
White craft glue
Flat head pliers

Instructions

———

1. Download and print the templates from www.bookhou.com/pages/embroidery-patterns. Transfer the template onto one piece of the linen. Since the linen I used wasn't too heavy I was able to transfer by putting the template underneath, holding it up against a window and tracing with a pencil (see page 18 for transfer techniques).

2. Stretch the linen piece onto your hoop (see page 21 for stretching instructions). Thread an arm's length of thread onto your milliner's needle and tie a quilter's knot (see page 22) at the end. I began by working on the flower petals using bullion stitch (see page 33) in rust (Warbler) and pale pink (Flesh). I worked each colour for two or three rows; changing the number from time to time gives the design a more organic feel. Also remember that, although you will be creating parallel rows of stitches, some rows will be different lengths with different starting points in order to maintain the curved shape of the petals. Go around each flower until all the petals are complete.

3. Now change to an embroidery needle and begin stitching the centre of the flowers with satin stitch (see page 38) in dark yellow. Start from the middle and extend to the start of the petals, going around in a circle until the centres are all filled in. Again, don't feel the need to make each stitch the same in length – this satin stitching will give the centre a nice texture that mimics the flower's pollen.

4. For the stem and the leaves I used stem stitch (see page 30) in army green only as an outline, without filling in the area. I felt that an outline alone wouldn't compete with the flower shape. Stem stitch has a nice twist, making it a good stitch to go with the bullion.

5. Once you have finished embroidering the front panel of the purse, cut it to the purse shape on the template and cut a back in the other piece of linen. Cut the same two shapes from the lining and interfacing pieces.

6. Place the backing and front with right sides facing each other and sew around the bottom portion with a 1cm (⅜in) seam allowance, starting and ending where the straight line connects with the curve. Repeat with the lining. Cut small snips into the seam allowance along the curve on the lining and main piece.

7. Turn the embroidered piece right sides out and push it inside the lining. Sew the main piece to the lining around each top 'flap' separately, using a 1cm (⅜in) seam allowance and leaving a 5cm (2in) gap at one top edge. Turn the purse right sides out through the gap.

8. Press the edge of the purse with an iron and set aside. Take the metal purse frame kit and cut the cord that comes with it so that it will fit around on the inside of the frame. Apply the white craft glue to the inside of the frame on one half only. Take one top 'flap' of the purse and push it inside one side of the frame – if the fit is a bit loose, fill the gap with the cord. Allow the glue to dry on this side first, usually a half hour. Then repeat on the other side. Once the glue has all dried it's an option to take the flat pliers and squeeze the metal slightly closed in the area close to the hinges on each side for extra security. I normally place a bit fabric over the metal frame when doing this so that the pliers don't dent the metal.

5.

6.

7.

8.

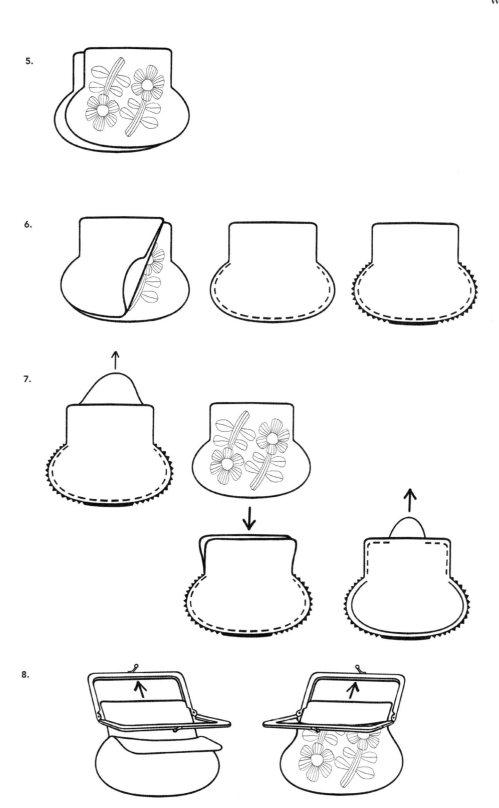

Goldwork brooch

———

I was pleased to be able to include a goldwork embroidery project in the book because it gives such an interesting result. Traditionally goldwork was used for special occasion garments and done with gold wire and bullion, which is made of fine coiled wire. The bullion comes in different sizes as well as different levels of shine. I chose to keep my bullion more on the matte side with a few shiny colours to give it some contrast. I worked on a black wool felt base because it doesn't fray, so the edges can be kept raw and cut close to the gold work, giving the piece a nice outline. This piece is finished with a pin back so you can wear it as a brooch, but feel free to sew it like a patch directly onto a jacket or sweater.

Skill level: Intermediate

YOU WILL NEED

Black wool felt

Needle and thread or white/silver permanent marker

18cm (7in) no-slip hoop

Bullion wire in a variety of colours (see Resources on page 142)

Black sewing thread

No. 6 embroidery needle

Scissors and snips

White craft glue

Metal sew-on pin backs

Instructions

──────

1. Place the felt in the hoop (see page 21 for stretching instructions). I tried a number of ways to transfer the image and I found the best way was to download and print out the template from www.bookhou.com/pages/embroidery-patterns onto plain paper and trace out the image lines with a tacking (basting) stitch. When I felt I had enough information down, I removed the paper leaving behind the stitches, which could either stay or be removed as you work. If you're more comfortable drawing free hand images on the black felt, using a white or silver permanent marker showed up the best (see page 18 for transfer techniques).

2. The main stitch that I used to hold down the bullion was a couching stitch (see page 39). If you pull the coils apart a tiny bit, the stitching falls in between them and so is unseen. To create the design, start by outlining the image. Refer to the stitch template for colour information.

3. After finishing the outline, proceed to work on the interior details. In some designs I covered more of the base cloth, but in most cases I left some of the black wool exposed. I think it makes the bullion stand out more with the contrast in colours and texture.

4. After the embroidery is finished, glue another layer of the same felt onto the back using white craft glue to cover all the embroidery threads on the back. Press it lightly with a weight until dry. Then trim the excess felt around the edges to the final shape, and sew on a pin back.

Scallop flat pouch

— — —

I love making small objects like pouches. They're quick to make and are the right size to showcase any type of design – and they are perfect for embroidery. This scallop image is designed as a repeat pattern with a subtle play of colour, which includes the indigo of the base cloth that is visible between the stitches. The finished pouch is 18 x 20cm (7 x 8in). The embroidery is very easy, so this would be a beginner's project if you stitched the design onto something ready-made.

Skill level: Intermediate

YOU WILL NEED

Sulky Stick 'n Stitch

25 x 30cm (10 x 12in) piece of indigo linen fabric

18cm (7in) no-slip hoop

DMC threads (floss) in yellow-green (3819), pine green (3364), silver-grey (318), grey-green (926), celadon green (3817)

No. 3 or 4 embroidery needle

Iron

20 x 23cm (8 x 9in) piece of indigo linen fabric

2 pieces of cotton calico (muslin) each 20 x 23cm (8 x 9in)

Scissors and snips

20cm (8in) indigo or black plastic zipper

Sewing machine with zipper foot and thread

Instructions

1. Download and print the template from www. bookhou.com/pages/embroidery-patterns to 14 x 20cm (5½ x 8in) onto Stick 'n Stitch and apply it in the middle of the larger piece of the indigo linen. If you don't have a printer you can transfer the image using another method (see page 18 for transfer techniques). Choose an area to start and stretch it onto the hoop (see page 21 for stretching instructions). I find that when you use a smaller hoop it holds the fabric more taut. If you find it easier to work with the fabric stretched on a larger hoop you can give that a try, but then you may need to make your base cloth a little larger.

2. Choose a colour to start, thread an arm's length of the first colour onto your needle and tie a quilter's knot (see page 22) at the end. The entire piece is done with split stitch (see page 30). Start in one corner of a scallop and stitch each line going back and forth until each area is filled, with about a stitch width of space between each line left empty. I find it easier to stitch each area of the same colour in the stretched hoop first before moving on to other colours – that way you are not switching back and forth between colours too often. Keep in mind that if you are stitching on top of the Stick 'n Stitch, you will need to try and keep your thread tension a little bit tighter so there won't be a gap between the stitching and base cloth when you dissolve the paper upon completion.

3. Once you have done all the stitching, take the embroidered piece and rinse it under warm water, gently rubbing the paper with your fingers. This will dissolve the Stick 'n Stitch, leaving the embroidery behind. Lay flat to dry. Once dried, iron the panel and then cut the panel to its final shape and size of 20 x 23cm (8 x 9in). You will be trimming the panel close to the embroidery with an additional 1cm (⅜in) all around for seam allowances. Refer to the template if necessary. The other piece of linen and the two calico pieces should be trimmed to the same size if necessary.

4. Lay the zipper facing up on the right side of one of the lining pieces with the outer edge of the zipper tape aligned along the long top edge and the zipper centred. Next, lay the embroidered front piece, right side facing down, on top of the zipper with the long top edge aligned with the zipper tape edge and lining below. Using a zipper foot, stitch along the edge with a 1cm (⅜in) seam allowance. Fold over both pieces of fabric along the finished zipper seam.

5. Repeat step 4 with the other two pieces of fabric, add the lining below the zipper and the plain back piece above it.

6. Lay the pouch flat and fold over the sides so that the two lining piece are now right sides facing inwards on one side of the zipper and the front and back of the pouch are right sides facing inwards on the other side of the zipper.

7. Sew around the entire edge with a 1cm (⅜in) seam, sewing slowly and carefully over the ends of the zip, leaving a 7.5cm (3in) opening on the long side of the lining to turn right side out. Clip all four corners of the fabric.

8. Open the zipper then turn the whole pouch right side out through the hole in the lining, and then stitch the opening in the lining closed with the machine or by hand. Push the lining inside the pouch. If necessary you can press the pouch with an iron.

3.

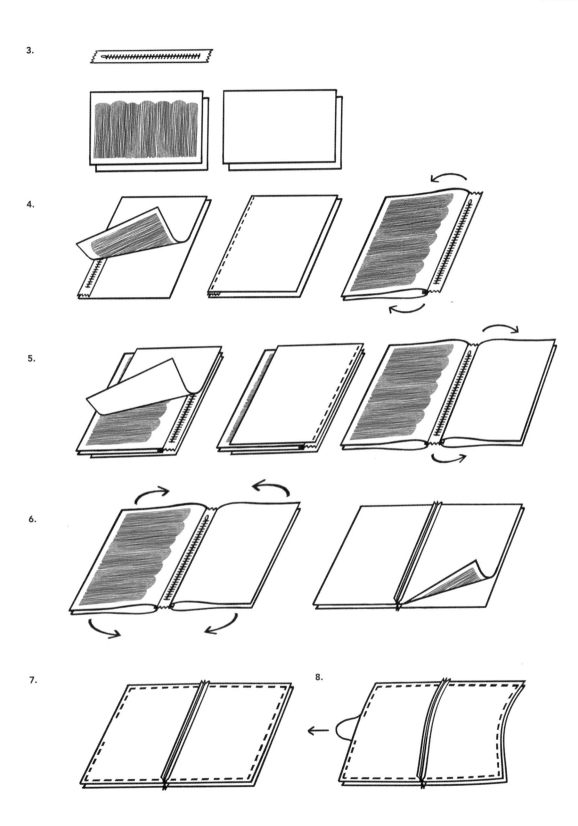

4.

5.

6.

7.

8.

Leaf crop top

———

Adding an embroidered motif to clothing is a great way to personalize your wardrobe and breathe new life into a well-loved garment. It's also the perfect way to update some older pieces rather than discarding them for something new. For this project you can use any existing shirt that you have to hand, but I thought it would be fun to sew up a crop top using a sewing pattern from Helen's Closet (see Resources on page 142). This crop pattern is very versatile – you can not only change the length, but also add short cap sleeves if you don't want a tank top. For the motif I was inspired by the Chinaberry leaf and I made sure it was quite big to showcase the shape of the leaves.

Skill level: Easy

YOU WILL NEED

Crop top sewing pattern

1.4m (1½yd) of cotton/linen blend fabric

Scissors and snips

Sewing machine – optional

Graphite transfer paper

Pencil

25cm (10in) embroidery hoop

Wonderfil Eleganza® perlé cotton thread (floss) #8 in Licorice (EZ05)

No. 7–10 embroidery needle

Iron

TIPS

Helen's Closet sells the crop top as a downloadable pattern. You can also use a pattern of your own, or an existing shirt or tee.

Choose a fabric that is somewhat opaque so the embroidery threads (floss) aren't visible on the back. I used a cotton/linen blend because it has a nice weight and level of opacity. Other fabrics would be fine as well, but try to use one that is light- to medium-weight so that it's not too heavy.

Instructions

———

1. If you are using a paper pattern for the crop top, prewash the fabric and sew the garment first according to the pattern instructions before starting the embroidery.

2. Download and print the template from www.bookhou.com/pages/embroidery-patterns, making sure to size it according to your garment. I wanted the image to be quite large so I made it 35.5cm (14in) tall. If you are printing out the template you can use a home printer and tile the pages so you can tape the pieces together.

3. Because the fabric I chose for the crop top is quite opaque it was difficult to see through so I chose to transfer the image using graphite transfer paper (see page 18 for transfer techniques). However, you could also draw it freehand.

4. I wanted the design of the leaf to have both a graphic impact and a certain simplicity. And since the leaves and stems already had such an interesting shape, I decided to keep the embroidery as a line drawing using only a back stitch (see page 29) with no filler stitches, worked in dark brown perlé cotton thread (floss). Thread the embroidery needle and tie a quilter's knot (see page 22) on the end. Since this is a garment, make starting and finishing knots that aren't too bulky and clean up any loose ends along the way so it's comfortable when wearing (see page 23 for the finishing knot). Press flat with an iron (see page 21).

5. Stretch a section of the image in your hoop (see page 21 for stretching instructions), and begin stitching the outlines of the leaf shapes and stems. Because I was working with a 25cm (10in) hoop I stitched in sections, completing each section before moving to the next as I moved my way around the design.

Fallen leaf tote

———

This bag design is simple to sew together, yet the fabric and embroidery give it a beautiful textural quality that really emphasizes the weight of the materials. The hemp canvas gives the bag a nice structure and is perfect for couching with wool yarn. While using a thicker thread like the yarn makes the stitching process faster, it also is a great way to showcase a repeat embroidery design that is composed of linear elements alone. The bag can be modified with longer straps to be carried on your shoulder or customized with interior pockets. It is great to carry all your essentials, or you can use it to carry around your embroidery projects in progress!

Skill level: Intermediate

YOU WILL NEED

0.5m (½yd) of hemp canvas or other medium-weight fabric

Scissors and snips

Transfer paper

Pencil

25cm (10in) no-slip hoop

50g (2oz) of aran (worsted) weight yarn in yellow

3 skeins of DMC thread (floss) in black (310)

No. 9 embroidery needle

Sewing machine and thread

0.5m (½yd) of cotton calico (muslin)

Heat-erasable pen

Iron

TIPS

I used hemp canvas for this bag, but drop cloth canvas will work too. You can also substitute something lighter in weight.

You can make the bag bigger or smaller if you like – just remember to allow for the seam allowance and the extra fabric for stretching when sizing your template.

Instructions

1. Download and print the template from www.
bookhou.com/pages/embroidery-patterns
to approx. 38 x 46cm (15 x 18in) and cut it
out – it already includes an additional 1cm
(⅜in) seam allowance. Place the template
on top of canvas with the transfer paper in
between facing down (see page 18 for transfer
techniques), making sure there is at least
7.5cm (3in) of extra fabric on all sides so there's
enough fabric for stretching. This extra fabric
will be trimmed afterwards. Using a pencil,
trace the shape of the bag onto the cloth.
When transferring on canvas you will have to
push a bit harder since the fabric is a bit thicker.

2. Once the image has been transferred, place the
fabric in the hoop (see page 22 for stretching
instructions). Start stitching using a couching
stitch (see page 39), completing all the stitches
within the hoop before moving the hoop to
a new location. I used a yellow yarn held in
place with black thread. You can leave a cut tail
underneath at the beginning and the end of the
yarn but it may fray over time, so a better way
to begin and end it is to fold the yarn end over
and secure it with the thread underneath as you
begin your couching. Likewise, when you run
out of a length of yarn, overlap the new piece
of yarn and stitch them down together so that
the thread line looks continuous. For the vein
of the leaf I used a split stitch (see page 30).

3. When the embroidered panel is complete, cut
the overall shape of the bag out, including the
1cm (⅜in) seam allowance. When cutting take
care to not trim any loose threads that may be
underneath. If you can't do that, use a sewing
machine and stitch around the edge of the
template shape first so that the stitching will
keep the embroidery from coming out. Cut an
additional piece of canvas the same size for
the back of the bag, and two pieces of cotton
calico (muslin), also the same size, for the lining.

4. Place the canvas exteriors right sides facing
each other and sew around the sides and
bottom leaving a 1cm (⅜in) seam allowance and
not sewing around the cut-out corners, which
will form a gusset. To sew the gusset, flatten
the bag across the bottom corners so the
edges of the cut-out are aligned and sew along
them. Place the two calico pieces together
and sew in the same fashion.

5. Turn the exterior canvas pieces right side out,
and place inside the calico lining so that the
seams and straps are all aligned. Join the
canvas and lining together by sewing along
the short curves on each side of the handle
with a 1cm (⅜in) seam allowance, leaving the
edges of all the handles unsewn (see diagram).
Similarly, join along the curves in the middle on
each side but leave a 7.5–10cm (3–4in) unsewn
gap along the bottom of one side. These gaps
will help you join the handles together and turn
the bag right side out.

6. At this point the handles are not attached.
Turn the bag right side out by pulling the
exterior out through the unsewn gap in the
middle of one side. Next push the lining so
that it's inside the bag. The bag will appear
almost complete but with the handles not
yet attached. Take the two inner ends of one
handle and sew along the top edge. Sew the
outer ends together so the seam is on the
inside. Repeat on the other handle.

7. Fold in the seam allowance along the raw
edges of both layers of each handle and press.
Sew a line of top stitching around all the bag
openings to join the two handle layers and
neaten all the edges.

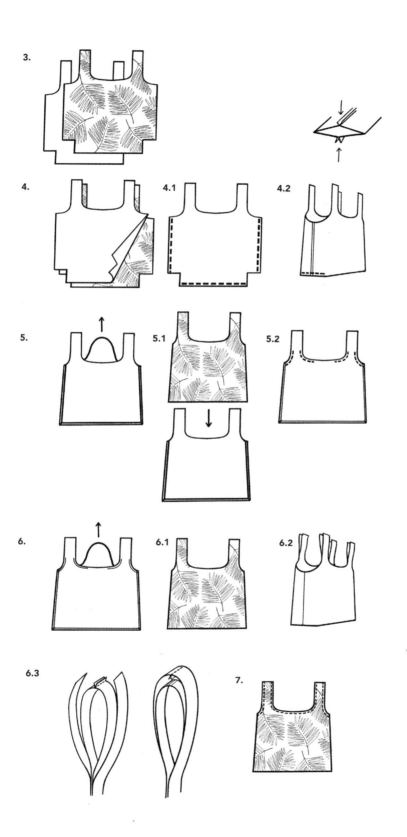

3.

4.   4.1   4.2

5.   5.1   5.2

6.   6.1   6.2

6.3   7.

Foliage cross-body bag

Embroidery is the perfect complement when working with other media, especially printed cloth. This small cross-body bag has a panel that was block-printed using pre-made wood blocks and a neutral coloured ink, and then embellished with stitchwork using a variety of stitches. There are a lot of possibilities for this project. You can use your own carved blocks, or print with found objects. You can stencil the images or simply paint on the fabric. Adding embroidery to the printed image gives it a different texture and refined detail to the lines.

Skill level: Intermediate

YOU WILL NEED

Scissors and snips

Istihome wood blocks and fabric ink, or any other blocks or stencils

Foam roller

25cm (10in) embroidery hoop

DMC thread (floss) in topaz (781), pale yellow (745), grass green (3363)

No. 3 or 4 embroidery needle

No. 7–10 embroidery needle

Overlocker (serger) – optional

Sewing machine and thread

Iron

15 x 20cm (6 x 8in) of piece hemp canvas

7.5 x 132cm (3 x 52in) strip of hemp canvas for the strap

25 x 30cm (10 x 12in) piece of hemp canvas

TIPS

I used a hemp canvas for this bag, but feel free to use what you have.

Before doing any printing or painting it's a good idea to wash the fabric so that all the sizing is removed. The ink is acrylic so there's no need to heat set the fabric; once it has dried it will not wash out.

I overlocked (serged) the interior so my bag doesn't have a lining, but feel free to cut two additional fabric pieces for the lining if you don't have an overlocker (serger).

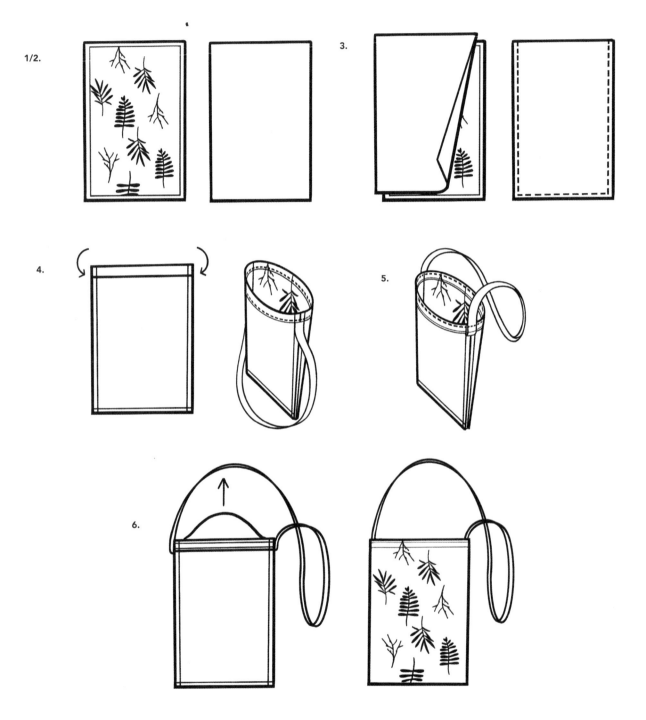

Instructions

1. Draw a 15 x 20cm (6 x 8in) rectangle in the middle of the largest piece of canvas, making sure there's enough extra around the edges so you can stretch it onto the hoop later. Lay the fabric flat on a table and print a random pattern using your blocks. I used wood blocks from Istihome and acrylic ink. To print, roll a small amount of ink onto a flat surface or plate using a foam roller. Roll ink onto one block and, using the tips of your fingers, press it onto the fabric. Apply even pressure and avoid using your palm as this may result in the block moving. Repeat two or three times before moving on to the next shape. Allow the ink to dry.

2. Stretch the printed fabric on a hoop (see page 21 for stretching instructions). Let the printed images help you to determine what details to add. The branch piece looked like there were buds so I added flowers using six strands of pale yellow and satin stitch (see page 38). For the some of the leaf shapes I added vein details using two strands of grass green and back stitch (see page 29). For other leaves I worked seed stitch (see page 45) in two strands of topaz. Just embroider enough to provide some detail, don't feel the need to cover the prints with too much embroidery.

3. Once you are finished with the embroidery, trim the front panel to 15 x 20cm (6 x 8in). Take the front and back pieces and overlock (serge) all edges of the fabric. You can also do a zigzag around the edges if you don't have an overlocker (serger). Place the two pieces together with right sides facing each other and sew all around the bag with a 1cm (⅜in) seam allowance, leaving the top of the bag unsewn.

4. Fold each long side of the strap to meet the middle, then fold the strap in half so the raw edges are concealed inside. Sew close to the edge along both folded edges. Fold over the top of the bag by 2.5cm (1in) all around and press. Place the ends of the strap under the folded flap on each side, with the loop hanging down, and then sew a line of top stitching all around the top edge of the bag just above the overlocking. This will attach the top flap to the bag and secure the straps.

5. Pull the loop of strap upwards so it is now coming up out of the sides of the bag. Sew another line of top stitching along the top edge close to the fold and across the straps.

6. Turn the bag right side out.

Rose cardigan
or sweater

———

Throughout history embroidery has always been connected with clothing for its ability to embellish and decorate. And it's still a great way to customize and personalize a garment or to bring new life to something that you might no longer be wearing. What I like about this project is it's a small addition that is nice and quick, but has a big impact.

Skill level: Intermediate

YOU WILL NEED

Sulky Stick 'n Stitch

Scissors and snips

Cardigan or sweater, new or used

18cm (7in) no-slip hoop (or bamboo hoop)

Wonderfil Ellana® wool threads (floss) in Old Gold (EN35), Artichoke Heart (EN11), Salmon (EN25)

No. 7–10 embroidery needle

TIPS

Either cotton or wool thread (floss) is fine for this project, or you can also use a heavier yarn – which would make the embroidery easier to do on a stretchy knitted fabric.

The hoop size is optional – you can use any size hoop you have.

Instructions

———

1. For this project I downloaded from <u>www.bookhou.com/pages/embroidery-patterns</u> and printed the flower template on Stick 'n Stitch, sized to 9cm (3½in) wide, and the leaves template a bit smaller. Cut out the design leaving an extra 5mm (¼in) all around the image, then peel and stick onto the area you want to embroider. Feel free to adjust the size of the image to suit the sweater that you are working with. If you don't have a printer you can use a fine permanent marker to trace the design onto the paper (see page 18 for transfer techniques).

2. Stretch the fabric over the hoop (see page 21 for stretching instructions). Remember, sweaters are a bit stretchier than woven cloth so make sure to not pull too tight in the hoop or you will distort the garment as you work. If the whole image doesn't fit on the hoop, choose a section and move the hoop when complete.

3. Thread an arm's length of the first colour into the needle and tie a quilter's knot (see page 22) at the end. See pages 27–47 for all embroidery stitch instructions. I started by embroidering the stem and leaves in back stitch and moved on to the flowers next. For the flowers I used satin stitch to divide the flower into sections, like a pie, before filling each section in with satin stitch. This will make it easier to achieve an even balance of stitches without any heavy areas.

4. When finished, hold the embroidered area under warm running water, gently rubbing the Stick 'n Stitch with your fingers. The paper will dissolve leaving the embroidery behind. Lay the sweater flat to dry on a towel.

Raised botanical hoops

——

Most embroidery stitches seem content to remain on the surface of the fabric, contributing to the design with colour and shape. But that is not always the case – many stitches can create incredible 3D textures, objects and forms. For this project I wanted to create a triptych with a botanical theme, with each panel expressing its own personality that goes beyond the surface. I didn't transfer an image onto the base cloth as with the other projects; instead I worked in a freeform manner, referring to the image template only for guidance.

Skill level: Advanced

YOU WILL NEED

3 wood hoops, each 18cm (7in) diameter

Black canvas fabric or any dark fabric

DMC thread (floss) in beige (3864), avocado green (471), mid-green (3347), taupe (372), yellow (3822)

DMC perlé cotton thread (floss) #8 in dark grey (3799)

Wonderfil Eleganza® perlé cotton thread (floss) #8 in Brass Trumpet (EZ17)

Black thread

No. 3 or 4 embroidery needle

Tapestry needle

15cm (6in) of 5mm (¼in) natural cotton rope

10cm (4in) of 5mm (¼in) yellow cotton rope

Scissors and snips

Round-head sewing pin

Instructions

———

1. Stretch a piece of canvas onto each frame (see page 21). Download and see the stitch templates at www.bookhou.com/pages/embroidery-patterns for the design outlines, and pages 27–47 for all embroidery stitch instructions. Thread an arm's length of thread onto a needle each time, and tie a quilter's knot (see page 22) at the end before beginning to stitch.

2. On hoop no. 1, the flowers have a tufted look from using Turkey work. Create a circle of loops with taupe thread on one half of the circle and another with beige thread on the other half. When finished, cut the top off the loops to create the tufts. Repeat for the other two flowers. For the stem cut a length from natural cotton rope of 5mm (¼in) to fit the diagram, then hold it in place with a couching stitch. Then use the mid-green thread to cover the rope by working a raised stem stitch in rows going up and down from one side to the other until the rope is completely covered.

3. For hoop no. 2, use a yellow cotton rope as the stem and hold it in place with a couching stitch in a black or dark grey contrasting thread. Once done, create leaves using the woven picot stitch. Make each leaf using avocado green 1.2cm (½in) wide and about 2.5cm (1in) long. I used three strands to create the weaving. I started from the bottom of the stem and moved my way around until all sides were covered with the leaves.

4. For hoop no. 3, start by creating the flower centre by taking a length of rope and coiling it to create a circle about 2cm (¾in) wide, holding it in place with a couching stitch. Then take a yellow cotton thread and sew around the edge of the coiled rope using back stitch to form a nice circular edge. Finally, cover the coiled natural rope with stitches to create a dome shape – I used blanket stitches, and kept stitching in a circular motion until it was covered. Next, surround the flower centre with petals using woven picot stitch in brass trumpet floss thread. I used only two strands to weave each petal so they were narrower, and created two rows of petals – the first layer was created with petals right beside each other, with the second layer underneath and in between the first row of petals. For the stems use a yellow cotton rope and make three rows in a back stitch, then use the same stitch in the avocado green to create an outline for the leaves. Fill in the leaves using weave stitch.

Oval bird frame

———

One of the most common, and enjoyable, things to create with embroidery is wall art. Because these are usually a little larger than other projects you have the freedom to really explore the potential of different stitches. I used an Auburn hoop to frame the finished piece and I really like how the design, with its curved branches, integrates with the oval shape of the hoop. For this piece I wanted the colours to move away from the usual greens that I gravitate towards. I think the colours chosen worked well with the pink linen base cloth; complete harmony.

Skill level: Easy

YOU WILL NEED

Approx. 30cm (12in) square of pink linen fabric

Heat-erasable pen

Pins or tape

25cm (10in) no-slip hoop

DMC thread (floss) in Ecru, black (310), coral (350), light terracotta (3778), dark blue-grey (924), grey-green (926)

Sajou Retors du Nord thread (floss) in Powder (2479)

No. 9 embroidery needle

Scissors and snips

15 x 20cm (6 x 8in) Auburn oval hoop in unfinished colour

Needle and thread

Instructions

1. Download and print the templates from www. bookhou.com/pages/embroidery-patterns with an image sized for your oval frame. If the fabric you are using is light in colour you can transfer the image by placing the printout underneath your fabric, using pins or tape to keep it in place, and holding it up to a window to trace (see page 18 for transfer instructions).

2. Next, stretch the fabric onto a hoop (see page 21 for stretching instructions). It is possible to work directly on the oval display hoop, but my design includes a branch that goes off the edge so I stretched the fabric on a larger no-slip hoop to work on. It can be transferred over to the oval hoop when it is done.

3. Choose a section to start, referring to the stitch template for the outline of the design – see pages 27–47 for all embroidery stitch instructions. Thread an arm's length of the first colour onto a needle and tie a quilter's knot (see page 22) at the end. Feel free to start wherever you like, but I started by filling in the branch with long and short stitches to give it a thick, strong presence. Afterwards, I worked the leaves using satin stitch. On the bird I used split stitch for the outlines and seed stitch on the body – I wanted the bird to stand out so I left it as a black line drawing. Lastly, the small round flowers were done with satin stitch, and the large flowers with long and short stitches to create a colour gradation reminiscent of shading. This gradation technique gives the flowers more depth and shape. I worked on the flowers one petal at a time but it might be faster to work with one colour at a time, starting with the lightest colour on the edge of the petals working towards the centre and ending with the darkest colour.

4. Once you are done with the embroidery, stretch the fabric onto the oval hoop according to the hoop directions. Trim any extra fabric on the back leaving a selvedge of 5cm (2in).

5. To finish the back, thread a needle, leaving the end unknotted. Sew a running stitch in the loose selvedge around the complete perimeter, just inside the frame.

6. When done, tie the two ends together and pull the thread taut, cinching the selvedge together. This can be trimmed further if necessary.

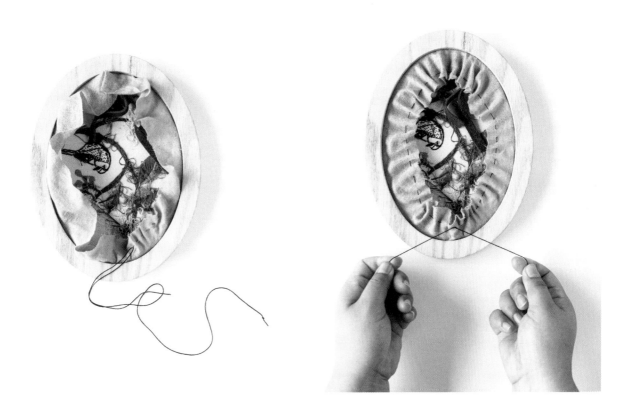

Nature book

——

One of the things I like to do on a daily basis is to draw or paint in my sketchbook; quite often little botanical images of leaves and flowers I've seen on walks, or imaginary ones I invented on my own. I thought how amazing it would be to make a fabric book of embroidery as an art piece, containing samples of the plant life that surrounds us.

Skill level: Intermediate

YOU WILL NEED

Sulky Stick 'n Stitch

Scissors and snips

Pencil

Piece of cotton calico (muslin) big enough to cut six rectangles each 11.5 x 20cm (4½ x 8in)

Heat-erasable pen

18cm (7in) embroidery hoop

Sajou Retors du Nord thread (floss) in Pine (2749), Ochre (2567), Moss (2034), Boxwood (2023), Olive (2445), Fern (2013), Pastel Green (2443), Undyed (2000)

No. 3 embroidery needle

Iron

14 x 25cm (5½ x 10in) piece of linen for cover

14 x 25cm (5½ x 10in) piece of cotton calico (muslin)

Sewing machine – optional

TIPS

For this project any type of fabric or remnants will work but I used cotton calico (muslin) for the pages. You can also use any type of fabric or remnant for the cover.

I used two strands of thread (floss) to give the piece a less bulky look but feel free to add more threads to make it go faster.

Instructions

1. Download and print the templates from www.bookhou.com/pages/embroidery-patterns, scaled to approximately 9cm (3½in) high; you can definitely scale them smaller or larger if you like. This project has lots of room for personal design, so print out to the scale you're comfortable with. I wanted to save time on transferring the images so I printed the template on Stick 'n Stitch, but you can transfer them using another method (see page 18 for transfer techniques).

2. Cut out the images on the Stick 'n Stitch, making sure to cut around the edges as close as possible.

3. Using a pencil draw six rectangles each 11.5 x 20cm (4½ x 8in) onto the cotton calico (muslin). These will be the pages with a central fold. This dimension includes seam allowances so when you draw them they can be right next to each other. Using the heat-erasable pen make two small marks at the top and bottom of each rectangle to indicate the central fold line, with each side measuring 11.5 x 10cm (4½ x 4in). On the far sides, left and right, measure 1cm (⅜in) for the seam allowance. Place one of the image stickers centred between the seam allowance and the central fold. Because you will be stretching the fabric on your hoop, it might be better to place only one image sticker at a time and embroider it before moving on to the next image.

4. Embroider the images. I didn't choose a particular order with placement, I thought it would be fun for you to create your own arrangement. I also chose a similar palette for each image to produce a unified look. On the PDF stitch template (www.bookhou.com/pages/embroidery-patterns) I have indicated the stitches I used as well as the colours, but you can use other colours and brands.

5. After you finish all the embroidery work, rinse the Stick 'n Stitch pieces one by one under warm running water, gently rubbing the paper with your fingers. When all the paper stickers have dissolved, lay the fabric flat and let it dry. Once dry, give the fabric a good pressing with an iron.

6. Moving to the linen cover, follow the same steps using the Stick 'n Stitch and once completed rinse off the paper and press with an iron.

7. Cut out the rectangular panels for the pages. Start by sewing the cover to the inside cover lining by placing them right sides facing each other and sewing around the perimeter with a 1cm (⅜in) seam allowance and leaving a 7.5cm (3in) unsewn gap opening on one of the long sides. Clip the corners, then turn right sides out. You can either stitch along close to the edge, which will close the opening, or press the cover and hand stitch to close the opening, which is what I did.

8. Set aside and begin sewing the pages of the book in pairs in the same way – you will end up with three double pages with embroidery on both sides. You can definitely add more pages if you like with different images or repeat some of the images but in a different colourway. Press all the pieces with an iron.

9. Stack the pages on top of each other and make sure they are in the order you want. Then lay everything flat on top of the inside of the cover (lining side). Make sure all pages are neatly aligned and centred on the cover. If you want you can pin down all the layers so they don't move. Stitch along the central line to create the fold, and the book is complete.

3.

4.

7.

7.1

7.2

7.3

8.

8.1

9

9.1

Foraged finds

———

Embroidery lends itself well to combinations of materials and media and in this project you can create a multimedia image with embroidery and photography. The flat-lay image of botanical samples is one of my photographs and is available for printing on Spoonflower (see page 142). But you can use one of your own photographs – just print it out at home using an image transfer product that is normally used for T-shirts. The important thing to keep in mind is that it is a collaboration between the existing image and what you stitch. Feel free to use any type of stitching you like, but try to allow the photograph's imagery to inform what types of stitches you use, the shapes you make and the colours you choose. Make sure that you are not completely covering up the printed image below by leaving spaces between stitches and not filling in areas.

Skill level: Intermediate

YOU WILL NEED

Fabric or paper with an existing image or you can print your image on fabric via Spoonflower or any other printer that provides a similar service

Wood stretcher frame, 30 x 35cm (12 x 14in) outside dimensions

Staple gun

DMC thread (floss) in chocolate brown (975), bright green (907), mid-green (3347), dark green (934), dark yellow (3820), taupe (372), light olive (734), light gold (422), golden brown (420), pistachio green (320)

No. 5 or 6 embroidery needle

No. 7–10 embroidery needle

Scissors and snips

TIPS

When working with three or four strands use a no. 5 or 6 embroidery needle, and with six strands use a no. 3 or 4 needle.

You can also do this type of embroidery on old postcards or other printed paper rather than fabric. In most cases, printed images already have some 3D quality, but stitching on top of the image gives the piece even more depth and a real magical quality.

Instructions

1. Begin by stretching your fabric onto a wood frame (see page 21 for stretching instructions) using a staple gun (if using paper you can skip this step). Wood frames can be purchased from any art supply store, similar to those painters use for stretching canvases, or can be made at home. If your fabric is too lightweight you may see the frame underneath, which was the case with the fabric that I had my image printed on. To compensate for this I put a layer of cotton calico (muslin) underneath the printed fabric to give it more opacity. This also gives the surface a bit more weight when stitching.

2. Referring to the stitch template for colour information, and starting from the upper left and moving clockwise, each leaf group was stitched as follows (see pages 27–47 for stitch instructions).

3. The green five-leaf stem has a striping effect using narrow satin stitches moving on a diagonal from each leaf's centre line to the outside edge, where it creates a jagged edge. The thread colour used was similar in colour to the printed image, giving it a nice tonal effect.

4. The brown leaf at the top is overlaid with a random circular pattern over the entire surface of the leaf using a back stitch. The stitch is a continuous line that meanders in circles, leaving open circular gaps to see the photograph beneath. The colour is brighter, but similar to that of the photograph below so as to appear as tones of textured patterning across the surface of the leaf.

5. The green leaf is embroidered with a central stem stitch forming the leaf stem, and is also covered across its entire surface with little seed stitches. The thread for the stem is similar to that of the photograph, giving it a slight 3D look, while the dashes are a lighter green creating a pattern effect.

6. For the large flower on the right hand side, three colours of yellow are stitched using French knots in a very random manner. The placement is based on light and dark flowers on the photograph. Using three colours also gave that area more depth. The leaves are left quite simple with a single split stitch at the centre, while the sides consist of single stitches, evenly spaced.

7. The group of leaves in the centre bottom is similar to those above with a stitching of fine, single stitches on the leaves, evenly spaced. The stems are a combination of stem stitches and a thin satin stitch. The red berries are left unstitched.

8. For the three little flowers at bottom left a blanket stitch is used to give the petals more detail. The stitch forms a border along the outside edges and each stitch extends to the centre of each leaf. I like how the blanket stitch gives the edge a nice border that was thicker, leaving a lot of the image exposed with the light and shadow giving more depth to the image.

9. Lastly, the group of leaves in the middle consists of split stitches in two colours running the length of the larger leaves, and lines of single stitches on the two smaller leaves that also contain a split stitch along their veins.

Alphabet sampler

I've always loved old embroidery samplers, and creating one is a perfect way to make a stitch library of sorts. Although most samplers contain alphabets, numbers and text, I decided to keep this one as only an alphabet but to make it with a variety of stitches, and use shapes and forms to create the letters in little compositions. This alphabet is about variety in design, and variety in stitches, where each letter is like a project in itself, completely different from any other. Because none of the letters are the same, I created a detailed chart on the stitch I used as well as colours and thread (floss) to guide you along the way (download the stitch template from www.bookhou.com/pages/embroidery-patterns). I mostly used Sajou and DMC thread, but for one of the letters I used Baker's twine and rope – feel free to substitute that with one of the embroidery threads if you like.

Skill level: Advanced

YOU WILL NEED

Approx. 38 x 43cm (15 x 17in) piece of light natural linen

Pencil or heat-erasable pen

25cm (10in) no-slip hoop

DMC thread (floss) in Ecru, lime green (166), olive green (733), mid-green (3347), dark green (934), dusky pink (152), red-brown (918), golden brown (975)

Sajou Retors du Nord thread (floss) in Gobelin Blue (2818), Emerald (2777), Agate (2876), Honey (2570), Navy (2864), Black (2005), Cloud (2001), Shetland (2705), Ash (2037), Powder (2479), Coral (2017), Warbler (2016)

20cm (8in) of 5mm (¼in) cotton cord

61cm (24in) of natural colour baker's twine

No. 3 or 4 embroidery needle

No. 5 or 6 embroidery needle

No. 7–10 embroidery needle

Scissors and snips

Wood stretcher frame, 30 x 35cm (12 x 14in) outside dimensions

---

TIPS

When working with six strands use a no. 3 or 4 embroidery needle, with three or four strands use a no. 5 or 6 needle, and with one or two strands use a no. 7–10 needle.

Instructions

——

1. Download and print the template from www.bookhou.com/pages/embroidery-patterns to 23 x 30cm (9 x 12in) and make sure you have an extra 12.5cm (5in) all around so that there's enough fabric to stretch. Each letter of the alphabet should be approx. 4.5cm (1¾in) tall with varying widths. You may make them a bit bigger but I wouldn't go much smaller. Transfer the letter images onto the linen by placing the template underneath and holding it up to a window and then tracing with a pencil or heat-erasable pen, or see page 18 for other transfer techniques.

2. Choose an area to start and stretch the fabric onto your hoop (see page 21 for stretching instructions). To begin working on individual letters refer to the PDF stitch template for colour and stitch information. See pages 27–47 for all embroidery stitch instructions. Thread an arm's length of the first colour onto a needle and tie a quilter's knot (see page 22) at the end. Feel free to change up the colours based on what you have to hand, and to change any of the details as you wish; use this piece as a way to experiment and practise your stitches.

3. To display my piece I made a wood frame 30 x 35cm (12 x 14in) and stretched the fabric over it (see page 21 for stretching instructions).

		S = sajou
S2818	D166	D = DMC
S2777	ecru	S2864
S2876	S2001	S2005
S2570	S2705	S2017
D733	S2037	S2016
D3347	D152	D918
D934	S2479	D975

Garden wall art

————

Creating wall art based on the theme of a garden, with different kinds of plant life, is a wonderful way to explore how colour, shape and texture can combine to form intricate compositions. Its appeal is in its sheer variety and its loose organic structure of curved patches of leaves and flowers, each different in appearance but all contributing to a lovely whole. This piece is stretched on a wood frame giving it a more formal look and it will brighten any room in your house.

Skill level: Intermediate

YOU WILL NEED

25 x 35cm (10 x 14in) outside dimension wood frame

46 x 56cm (18 x 22in) piece of linen fabric

Staple gun

Pencil or water-soluble pen

DMC thread (floss) in black (310), dark avocado green (936), olive (830), hunter green (3345), pine green (3364), pale green (3348), dark blue-grey (924), light topaz (783), gold (676), terracotta (356), dark brown (400), mid-pink (758), pale pink (948), mid-grey (452), light grey (648)

Sashiko thread in white

Baker's twine

No. 7–10 embroidery needle

Scissors and snips

TIPS

I used 2.5cm (1in) square wood strips nailed and glued at the corners to make my frame, but slightly larger strips will do as well.

Instructions

———

1. Start by stretching the linen onto the wood frame (see page 21 for stretching instructions). Make sure it's quite tight as you'll be adding a lot of stitches.

2. Download and print the template from www. bookhou.com/pages/embroidery-patterns, making sure to size the image for the inside of the frame – approx. 20 x 25cm (8 x 10in). Transfer the image by placing it underneath the linen, holding them up to a light source such as a window, and tracing the image onto the linen with a pencil or water-soluble pen (see page 18).

3. Choose a section to begin the embroidery. Referring to the PDF stitch template for colour and stitch information, thread an arm's length of the first colour onto your needle and tie a quilter's knot (see page 21) at the end. Work on each patch at a time before moving on to the next. See pages 27–47 for all embroidery stitch instructions – most of the elements are achieved using satin stitch, with the exception of the patch of linear leaves at the bottom in split stitch, a series of single straight stitches for the blue daisy-like flowers and couching stitches for the middle arches and on the branching stems top left.

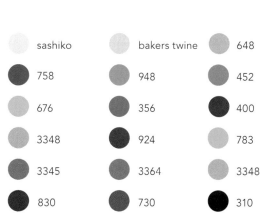

○	sashiko	○	bakers twine	●	648
●	758	●	948	●	452
●	676	●	356	●	400
●	3348	●	924	●	783
●	3345	●	3364	●	3348
●	830	●	730	●	310

Resources

DMC
dmc.com
Cotton threads (floss), transfer paper,
bamboo hoops, fabric

APPLETON WOOLS
appletons.org.uk
Wool threads (floss)

WONDERFIL
wonderfil.ca
Threads (floss) – cotton and wool
Wool felt

SAJOU
sajou.fr/en
Threads (floss) – cotton and wool

STUDIO CARTA
studiocartashop.com
Scissors

SULKY
sulky.com
Stick 'n Stitch

SPOONFLOWER
spoonflower.com
Digital-printed fabric

BOOKHOU
bookhou.com
No-slip hoop, needle minder

AVERY
avery.ca
Photo transfer paper

CLOVER
clover-mfg.com
Seam ripper, chalk pencil, iron-on
transfer pencil, water-soluble pencil

HOOPS
auburnhoops.co
Oval hoop

HAND & LOCK
handembroidery.com
Goldwork bullions

ART BASE
etsy.com/shop/artbase
Mini wood hoops

BLOCK PRINTING
istihome.com/en/shop/
Wood blocks and ink

MERCHANT AND MILLS
merchantandmills.com
Fabric

HELEN'S CLOSET
helensclosetpatterns.com
Ashton Crop Top and other
downloadable patterns

TEMPLATES
Download and print the templates from:
bookhou.com/pages/embroidery-patterns

Acknowledgements

———

Thank you to everyone at Quadrille Craft especially to Harriet Butt for being so supportive and to Alicia House for designing a beautiful book. Thank you also to Marie Clayton for editing my words.

Thank you to the talented Lauren Kolyn for capturing the projects so beautifully and the wonderful Lynda Felton for bringing the projects to life with your lovely styling beauty.

Thank you to Miyako, Rose and Piper for modelling.

To all the people who support me from near and far, my dear friends, my amazing mum Sengchanh and the Booths, and all of you who follow my process on social media – your positive energy makes my everyday brighter <3

To my children Lliam and Piper, you two are my heart and I love you both dearly.

A big thank you and lots of love to John for your endless support in life and business and for helping me make sense of my words; without you by my side none of this would be possible xx

About the author

Arounna Khounnoraj is a Canadian artist and maker working in Toronto, the city she emigrated to with her family from Laos at the age of four. While her education includes a master's degree in fine arts in sculpture and ceramics, her experiences eventually led to a career in fibre arts – where she focused on a range of printing techniques for textiles, as well as embroidery, patchwork and punch needle. In 2002 she started bookhou with her husband John Booth, a multi-disciplinary studio where she creates utilitarian textile objects such as bags, homegoods and textile art.

Arounna has explored a wide range of techniques, methods and materials that express a passion for everyday creativity and the importance of the handmade in everyone's life. Her work emphasizes slow design, intuitive thinking and the importance of handwork. She teaches workshops on a variety of fibre arts and crafts, both in Canada and internationally. She also collaborates with magazines, blogs and artists in creating social media and DIY projects. Arounna has previously published *Punch Needle* (2019) and *Visible Mending* (2020) with Quadrille.

Managing Director Sarah Lavelle
Senior Commissioning Editor Harriet Butt
Designer Alicia House
Photographer Lauren Kolyn
Stylist Lynda Felton
Head of Production Stephen Lang
Production Controller Katie Jarvis

Published in 2022 by Quadrille,
an imprint of Hardie Grant Publishing

Quadrille
52–54 Southwark Street
London SE1 1UN
quadrille.com

Cataloguing in Publication Data: a catalogue record for this book is available from the British Library.

Text and designs © Arounna Khounnoraj 2022
Photography © Lauren Kolyn 2022
Design and layout © Quadrille 2022

Reprinted in 2023
10 9 8 7 6 5 4 3 2

ISBN 978 1 78713 831 5

Printed in China using soy inks